AGENDA

Callings

AGENDA

CONTENTS

EDITORIAL   5

SPECIAL FEATURE

Feast of Fools: a collaboration inspired by   7
medieval Misericords
Stuart Henson, poet
Bill Sanderson, artist

ESSAY

William Bedford: Seamus Heaney: Out of the Marvellous   18

POEMS

James Roberts:	Cry Curlew	24
Jane Lovell:	Fugitive in the Date Palm	25
Diana Brodie:	Bringing Back Birdman	27
Jessamine O'Connor:	Snowbird	28
Ralph Monday:	Blackbird Testament	29
Eleanor Hooker:	Atomy of Deceit Lucid Dreaming	30
Will Stone:	Barn Owl	32
Lia Brooks:	Borstal The North in May – A Suite	33
Paul Murray:	On Hearing a Recently Deceased Singer on the Radio	37
Martin Bennett:	Balkan Busker, Metro A, Rome	38
John Gladwell:	Zero Gravity	39
Jeffrey Joseph:	Intimation	40

Hugh McMillan:	The Visitation: Jacob Epstein	41
Gill Learner:	Aural History What Love can do	42
Richard Ormrod:	Hands	44
David Cooke:	Empathy	46
Caroline Price:	To Iken and back Tutu	47
Stuart A Paterson:	Ebb And Flow Fire After Midnight	49

REVIEWS

Patricia McCarthy:	Not just Coffee Table books	50
Jonathan Barker:	'Break the lavender stem, and recorded time' *A C H Sisson reader*	56
W S Milne:	Nature's Prism	59

POEMS

Tony Curtis:	Two Poems i.m. Elizabeth Bishop House Self-Portrait Nude with Lota	64
Mario Petrucci:	Frau Beckmann	67
David Ball:	In the Hotel Negresco	68
David Pollard:	The Dark Fiddler Britten	69
Roland John:	Bombed-Out	71
Angela Croft:	Waving	72
Caroline Smith:	Mr Giang	73
Dan MacIsaac:	Torrington	75
Sue Mackrell:	Singing Their Way to the Ancestors Bred in the Bone	76
Howard Wright:	The Gritter Marina	79

Omar Sabbagh:	Fathers	80
Julie-ann Rowell:	Rocking Horse	81
Noel King:	Timoleague Fête	82
Robyn Rowland:	Garavogue Session	83
Terry McDonagh:	On the Train to Dublin, July 1st 2014	84
Kate Hendry:	Moving On Dreaming You Want Me Back	86
Gill McEvoy:	Where Are the Men?	88

CHOSEN BROADSHEET POETS

Francoise Harvey:	My love plays the fiddle on Southbank At Canada Water Life finds a way The Understudy	89
Jon Bridge:	On Carrownisky	92
Luke Palmer:	Two Births	94

NOTES FOR BROADSHEET POETS

Interview with **Kathryn Maris** by **Simon Collings**	96
Kathryn Maris: Two Poems	103
Ed Reiss reviews **Zaffar Kunial**, a Faber New Poet, 2014	105

BIOGRAPHIES   108

Front cover painting: **Alice Pickering** :
'The Conference of Birds' part of a triptych loosely based on the 12th century Sufi poem of that name that describes the difficulties and rewards of venturing away from one's own territory and setting out to explore the unknown.

Editorial

Thank you to contributors, subscribers and readers of this Spring issue of *Agenda*.

As we are doing the subscription service in-house now, please make sure you **renew your subscriptions as promptly as possible**. Also do watch out for renewal reminders by email and letter.

Don't forget to check in to **our website** www.agendapoetry.co.uk for new poems, paintings, essays/reviews, and for our online Broadsheets for young poets and artists, new sound-bites and archive materials. Also of course *Agenda*'s own book shop.

Calling all **YOUNG POETS** for the special double young Poets' issue of *Agenda* at the end of the year.

Next issue: '**Family Histories**': a general anthology, late summer.

A collaboration inspired by medieval Misericords between
Stuart Henson, poet and Bill Sanderson, artist

Feast of Fools

Misericords, the tip-up seats found in the Gothic choir stalls of churches and cathedrals in England and elsewhere in Western Europe, provide a rich and often humorous insight into the everyday world of the medieval craftsmen who carved them. Their purpose was humble – to allow the monks and priests a little relief from the strain of standing through a succession of long services – so the corbels were often decorated with images of labour, sport, domestic life or scenes from popular tales and fables. Just as the original carvings were freely adapted from sources such as the *Biblia Pauperum*, the poems draw their inspiration from particular misericords, in Beauvais, Ely and St David's among others, and the scraperboard illustrations take imaginative flight from the poems.

Ark

poor Noah
adrift in your bunker your
castle on the flood

turning through clouds
the interminable aftermath
as the wind exhales

sickened by groans of animals
each day
a little further out

like Major Tom
your eye rimmed by the light
in the telescope

its white bisected disc
quivering for something
tiny as a dove

Boat Builders / St Govan's Journey

swan-shaved
a fine curve of oak-grain
breasting the wave

then boat is the brine-bound belly
womb that will birth
on some far-flung shore

sawdust and resin
shed floor
of curled incense

blessed against
all fishy hatreds
whirlpond and hail-swarm

into our hands saint
stake
your mortality

nothing twixt soul
and nothing
but this tight form

pray for us now
and each dawn
when the prow leaps sunward

pray when you kiss the earth again
safely
in Rome

Dice Players

the ale-house is sweaty
with winter heat
a hive of chatter

drowsy with smoke and nectar
the hearthstone glows
and the pots remember

hops and dry barley
and in the snug the smatter
of boxwood and ebony

where numbers
tumble like acrobats
to the brink of probability

so their night rolls on
and its emptiness swells
through the gut of the fen-country

at the foot of the year's dark cross
they've already lost
in life's lottery

Green Man

so I utter
          leaves

furling like breath
          from the lungs of the earth

all the long vines
          and their green hands

coiling from memory

I am time
          I am ring upon ring

I am DNA
          in the helix of spring

I am speech
          I am whispering

I am one cell

          at the tongue-tip of being

Toothache

the pain
is bigger than him
midden-mouthed
and muscular
with a torturer's grin

raised
on those blue-green
images of sin
the damned
skewered at the Resurrection

he cries
mercy from everything anything
angel or Ahriman
dentist
or demon

whose surgery
is blood-floored and vicious
jaw-splintered
nauseous
excruciating

William Bedford

Seamus Heaney: Out of the Marvellous

Seamus Heaney: *New Selected Poems: 1966-1987* (Faber, 1990)
Seamus Heaney: *New Selected Poems: 1988-2013* (Faber, 2014)

With the work of a poet as diverse and ambitious as Heaney, one is going to find evidence of growth and development over a creative lifetime of fifty years, but I would like to focus on two issues which seem to me to be of continuous interest throughout his work: his response to the cultural and political crises he was born into, and his use of the circumstances of his personal life to reflect something deeper than the purely personal. In a body of work where readers are drawn irresistibly to analogy and allegory, it is often difficult not to see the personal and the political even in mythic material – most notably in *North, Sweeney Astray and Sweeney Redivivus* – but the simplest descriptive language can also take on figurative significances, as with the 'curt cuts' through 'living roots' of 'Digging.' There are clearly moments in Heaney's career when there is a heightening of intensity in both the political and spiritual concerns, but the concerns are there from the beginning.

Good titles resonate, but they can be limiting as well as illuminating. For anybody with a farming background, *Death of a Naturalist, Door into the Dark* and *Wintering Out* all bring to mind rural practices opaque to the urban reader, *Door into the Dark* making the most obvious leap into larger figurative possibilities. The earliest poems in these volumes amply justify the terms of the generous critical response, Douglas Dunn finding them 'loud with the slap of the spade and sour with the stink of turned earth'[1]; Neil Corcoran celebrating the kind of onomatopoeia and 'sheer noise' of 'the squelch and slap / Of soggy peat' and 'plash and gurgle of the sour-breathed milk' [2]; Christopher Ricks warning that after *Door into the Dark* Heaney would 'have to reconcile himself' to being seen 'as the poet of muddy-booted blackberry-picking' [3]. *New Selected Poems: 1966-1987* also includes from *Death of a Naturalist* 'Follower,' the most successful of

---

[1] Ed. Bernard O'Donoghue, *The Cambridge Companion to Seamus Heaney* (Cambridge University Press, 2009) p.3.
[2] Neil Corcoran, *The Poetry of Seamus Heaney: A Critical Study* (Faber & Faber, 1998) p.2.
[3] *The Cambridge Companion to Seamus Heaney*, ibid.

Heaney's many poems about his father and the reversal of roles in parent-child relationships, and 'Mid-Term Break,' the moving elegy for his four-year-old brother Christopher. What it excludes is 'For the Commander of the Eliza' and 'Docker,' an exclusion justifiable on critical grounds, but perhaps misleading in disguising an early engagement with the politics of Northern Ireland with its largely Protestant dockyard workers, and the awareness that 'That fist would drop a hammer on a Catholic - / Oh yes, that kind of thing could start again.' Happily, 'Personal Helicon' is included, with its final line – 'I rhyme / To see myself, to set the darkness echoing' – taking us straight into *Door into the Dark*, where we are, as often in Heaney, to some extent in the world of Hardy and Lawrence, but also, in 'Requiem for the Croppies,' the first successful expression of the poet's own political feeling. It might also be said that in the final poem in *Door into the Dark*, 'Bogland,' the last line's figurative reach – 'The wet centre is bottomless' – opens many doors into the historical and approaching darknesses of *Wintering Out*. Neil Corcoran was one of the few critics who recognised *Wintering Out* as one of Heaney's most significant collections. The pared-down line is certainly new, an austere form perhaps resisting the stereotyped clichés beginning to shape around his reputation. What is also new is the use of *dinnseancha*s, an old Irish form of the poetry of locality, explored most usefully in Bernard O'Donoghue's *Seamus Heaney and the Language of Poetry*.[4] 'Anahorish' and 'Broagh' have become famous examples of what Heaney was after here. *New Selected Poems: 1966-1987* leaves out the dedication, 'For David Hammond and Michael Longley,' which makes explicit reference to the political situation in Northern Ireland, but the relevance can hardly be missed in references to Edmund Spenser and 'geniuses who creep / "out of every corner / of the woodes and glennes"' in 'Bog Oak,' or in 'in the shared calling of blood // arrives my need / for antediluvian lore' from 'Gifts of Rain.' The promise 'Some day I will go to Aarhus' in the opening line of 'The Tollund Man' now seems to point to the inevitable direction Heaney was going to take, but must have been an obvious sign to informed readers even at the time.

Published in 1975, *North* was Heaney's most controversial collection, but in attempting to deal with his own experience as a Catholic living in Northern Ireland, he was never going to escape controversy. His move from Belfast to Wicklow in 1972 gave ample scope to sectarian resentment and accusation. He was supported by major figures such as Lowell, but without actually making the charge himself, Ciaran Carson repeated the

---

[4] Bernard O'Donoghue, *Seamus Heaney and the Language of Poetry* (Harvester Wheatsheaf, 1994).

claim that in writing *North*, Heaney had made himself 'the laureate of violence – a mythmaker, an anthropologist of ritual killing'[5]. The reference to anthropology derives from one of the sources of *North*, P.V. Glob's *The Bog People*. Describing, with photographs, the exhumations of prehistoric victims of ritual killings in Jutland, Heaney found here a mythopoeic framing which allows him to talk simultaneously about the victims Glob unearths, the news 'of each neighbourly murder', and the coffins in 'Funeral Rites' which he has helped to lift in his own family and community life. The pared-down forms created in *Wintering Out* are perfect for this material, and one finds it difficult to imagine that given time, anybody could object to the ambivalence straining for expression in 'Punishment,' where it is impossible to locate historically the victim with her 'shaved head / like a stubble of black corn, / her blindfold a soiled bandage, / her noose a ring // to store / the memories of love.' 'Punishment' is writing which attempts 'to say what happened' through the medium of myth. But *North* also takes up Lowell's challenge – 'Yet why not say what happened?'[6] – in the language of his Derry childhood and a transparent, almost journalistic, recording of his adult experience. 'Mossbawn: Two Poems in Dedication' are among his most popular elegies of childhood, whereas 'Whatever You Say Say Nothing' and the sequence 'Singing School' deal explicitly with his dilemma as a writer responsible to his polis but struggling to defend the rights of the imagination. Mandelstam is here in 'Exposure,' a stunningly beautiful rendering of this dilemma, caught in the winter peace of Wicklow. Heaney may have moved from Belfast, but his imagination remained firmly rooted in the North.

Heaney has talked of a kind of insouciance in the language of *Field Work*, published in 1979, but such insouciance cannot disguise the seriousness and immense ambition of these poems. 'Triptych' and 'The Toome Road' acknowledge the minority community's dilemma explicitly, the poet asserting 'I had rights-of-way, fields, cattle in my keeping' in countryside where foreign soldiers travel 'down my roads'. Yet he is helpless to defend the 'invisible, untoppled omphalos' of his land. In two of his greatest and most famous elegies – 'The Strand at Lough Beg' and 'Casualty' – death moves much closer to the poet's immediate family and community, with ritual killings and cleansings. There is a delicacy here in the gesture of 'cold handfuls of the dew / To wash you, cousin' when the washing is all too late, and will indeed be challenged later in *Station Island*. There is also a sort

---

[5] *The Cambridge Companion to Seamus Heaney*, ibid, p.4.
[6] Robert Lowell, 'Epilogue', *Day by Day* (Farrar, Straus and Giroux, 1992) p.127.

of guilt, in 'Casualty,' over 'Our tribe's complicity', the victim – 'Dawn-sniffing revenant, / Plodder through midnight rain' turning to 'Question me again', about his own role in the tragedy. The sequence 'Glanmore Sonnets' seizes the rural peace of Wicklow with an almost combative assertion of the rights of the English sonnet, Heaney rhyming in iambic pentameters as if the innovations of Modernism had never happened. A 'deep no sound / Vulnerable to distant gargling tractors' fills these poems, 'Thunderlight on the split logs' and the music of daily happening offered as solace and consolation for the horrors of history's nightmares. Especially interesting for what I am arguing about the continuities in Heaney's work is 'The Harvest Bow,' with its resonant 'Gleaning the unsaid off the palpable' foreseeing the themes of *Seeing Things*.

Published within the same couple of years, *Sweeney Astray* (1983), *Station Island* (1984) and *Sweeney Redivivus* (1984) question what some critics took to be the 'easy' consolations of *Field Work*, often accusing Heaney of pastoral nostalgia. It is almost impossible not to hear Heaney himself talking in some of the Sweeney poems. From *Sweeney Astray*, a 'little timorous stag / like a scared musician // startles my heartstrings / with high homesick refrains' in 'Sweeney Praises the Trees', while 'I would live happy / in an ivy bush / high in some twisted tree / and never come out', 'Sweeney Astray' tells us. Most explicitly, in *Sweeney Redivivus*, 'The First Flight' has the famous lines: 'I was mired in attachment / until they began to pronounce me / a feeder off battlefields,' one of the allegations being thrown around at the publication of *North*. Again, famously in *Station Island*, Heaney has the ghost of Colum McCartney – the victim of sectarian killing elegised in 'The Strand at Lough Beg' – return with his own accusation: that the poet '"confused evasion and artistic tact"' and thus '"saccharined my death with morning dew."' We go deeply underground – in Dante and Virgil's sense – with *Station Island*, but in the final poem of the sequence, it is Joyce who guides our poet, telling him 'it's time to swim // out on your own and fill the element / with signatures on your own frequency'. Several critics were puzzled by this, as this is precisely what Heaney had seemed to be doing with *Field Work*. *The Haw Lantern* was widely seen as an interim and less ambitious collection after the major creative achievements of *North* and *Field Work*, 'Alphabets' returning to a search for the roots of language acquisition, 'Clearances' echoing the music of earlier family elegies. 'The Wishing Tree' with its 'vision' of 'turned-up faces where the tree had stood' might be the exception, like 'The Harvest Bow' in *North,* foreseeing the themes of *Seeing Things*.

Whether or not 'there is no next-time-round,' the major sequence 'Squarings' in *Seeing Things* clearly attempts to express a new sense of the transcendent and visionary. 'Squarings' is divided into four sections – 'Lightenings,' 'Settings,' 'Crossings' and 'Squarings' of twelve-lined poems of four stanzas – much concerned with various crossings and thresholds. Bernard O'Donoghue has argued brilliantly that the very movement of the language from the opacity of the early volumes to the transparency of the language here 'is the most universal crossing of all' because it is to do with the transference or translation of meaning, the superb 'viii' from 'Lightenings', the monks of an abbey having a vision of the divine as a ship floating over their prayers, and a man desperately climbing down to their world to try and free the ship. The monks help him in his task, and he climbs back 'Out of the marvellous as he had known it.' Heaney took *Out of the Marvellous* as the title for his 2009 RTÉ documentary, and explains the incident as a sort of Orpheus experience, presumably the poet climbing down into the world around us, but finding the language to express his experience of the 'marvellous'. 'Squarings' is full of crossings of water and returns of the dead, but also in 'vi' and 'vii' from 'Lightenings' two wonderful stories about the child Hardy 'down on all fours' among the sheep, 'Charon's boat under the faring poets' in 'xxxvi' at the end of 'Lightenings,' the flash of police torches like fireflies accompanying protestors also in 'xxxvi'. I've quoted only from 'Lightenings' because the whole sequence is too rich to be read in quotation. *Seeing Things* also has wonderful revisits to Glanmore, and great individual poems such as 'Markings,' 'Man and Boy' with its thematic 'Blessed be down-to-earth!', 'Seeing Things' with its 'Sunlight, turfsmoke, seagulls, boatslip, diesel,' and the poem which precedes 'Squarings,' 'Fosterling,' where Heaney introduces his theme: 'Me waiting until I was nearly fifty / To credit marvels.'

The Spirit Level (1996) and *Electric Light* (2001) announce the continuing themes in their titles, and as always with Heaney contain justly famous poems. Given what I have been trying to say about the dangers of emphasising a radical change with *Seeing Things*, it is interesting also to see the number of poems which return to old scenes and themes. From *The Spirit Level*, 'A Sofa in the Forties' returns to the poet's Derry childhood; 'Two Lorries' has a journey then and now, with all the historic changes; 'Keeping Going' honours the determined 'keeping going' of the poet's brother; 'from The Flight Path' reminds us of the Long Kesh 'dirty protest'; 'Cassandra' in 'Mycenae Lookout' graphically reminds us of the shocking details of 'Punishment' in *North*; 'Tollund' deliberately takes us back to the 'Jutland fields' which so outraged some of Heaney's Belfast critics; perhaps in 'At the Wellhead' all of this reminds us that these experiences are the inspirational source, the groundbase, of Heaney's experience. In *Electric Light*, the last line of 'Perch' celebrates 'the everything flows and steady go of the world'; 'Out of the Bag' returns to the room where the Heaney children were born, the place of 'pure reality where I stand alone'; 'Book-learning is the thing' in 'Glanmore Eclogue' that might echo the country wisdom Heaney heard as a boy about to go off to boarding school; 'Bodies and Souls' revisits long-ago schooldays. 'Postscript,' the final poem in *The Spirit Level*, beautifully places the poet in both the material and the transcendent, caught between the earth and sea, in the 'neither here nor there', a familiar placing of the transcendent.

District and Circle (2006) and *Human Chain* (2010) came as late gifts, and include some of Heaney's greatest poems, not least the Hardyesque 'The Blackbird at Glanmore' from *District and Circle,* one of the finest poems of the last century. The excitement and consolation of reading these two volumes, is to experience again the evolving of a lyrical and ethical intelligence at work in history and language. Heaney's dwelling in the past has irritated some critics, but for me, his awareness of the past brings Wordsworth and Hopkins as close to us as Eliot and Hughes, the community of the living and the dead. One of the most astonishingly achieved and moving of these late poems is 'In the Attic,' where the poet remembers his childhood reading of *Treasure Island*, in the light of his current experience as an old man, 'As my uncertainty on stairs / Is more and more the lightheadedness // Of a cabin boy's first time on the rigging, / As the memorable bottoms out / Into the irretrievable, // It's not that I can't imagine still / That slight untoward rupture and world-tilt / As a wind freshened and the anchor weighed.' That we remember such glimpses of the visionary, and so much else, is due not least in part to the work of Seamus Heaney.

James Roberts

Cry Curlew

After a howling winter no return.
A man listens at upland pools
tunnelling beneath the susurration
of spike-rush and voiceless springs
as if their calls could only
be located beyond his hearing
scorched through a clot of emptiness.
The whorl of a polar night sea
will not echo across summer,
played on a white bone flute.
Will he forget them now,
the shock of that first call
on a distant March dawn
battering him with his own fragility,
forget that all living is a sudden
flare followed by a trailing note?

Jane Lovell

Fugitive in the Date Palm

It is hard to ignore the red-billed toucan.
Solomon says his bill is chipped like an old teacup
but we see the translucence of the *deglet noor*,
its caramelised sunlight.

After the stripping of thorn and billowing
of pollen across the plantation,
he blew in on a salt wind through the canyons,
beak bright as paintpots,

took shelter in the branches,
peeped at us with his blue eye from the canopy
while donkeys grazed determinedly below
oblivious to his dipping and tilting.

Solomon says he's an escapee from a sultan's
menagerie; we feed him pomegranate, mango,
leaving them in quiet acts of worship
at the foot of his favourite palm.

We know he is lonely, thousands of miles
of desert and ocean from home.
We call to him while we hang on ladders
wrapping the *khlal* in muslin.

Evenings, he hops about chuntering
at shadows, then curls into a feathered ball
secured by his great beak,
to sleep.

We think he dreams deep jungle:
Costa Rican mists, the whirring of moths
and pop of frogs, another red-billed toucan
hidden, waiting, in the forest gloom.

Solomon says one day, maybe he'll set off
like a beacon, winging over Egypt, Libya,
Nigeria, the South Atlantic.
He prays for the fruits to ripen,

sweet *rutab* to delay his leaving,
checks on him each morning, peering
up into the leaves, his crippled toes sinking
in the warm sand.

Note:
The terms *khlal* and *rutab* refer to stages in the ripening of the *Deglet Noor* date.

Diana Brodie

Bringing Back Birdman

Behind the iridescence
of his paua shell eyes,
beneath the *moko* carved
and painted on his chin,
skeletons of tiny birds
shift and settle in his head,
bring bone-rattle
        to the skies.

We watch over him. Men
file across wet sands, drop
beside the kite a heap
of clattering cockle shells,
tie them to his tail as weights.
'Oh Tawhirimatea!
god who moves the winds,
        may they rise!'

The god replies. Gusts ruffle
green *kaka* feathers sewn
to Birdman's barkcloth chest.
He breathes. Trembles. Ready
to head skywards as we chant:
'Ascend on high, Tāwhaki!
Go to the first, then
to the second heaven!'

What does it matter
if Birdman's music
is only bone-song,
shell-chatter? Look up!
        he flies!

Note:
Kites were a feature of New Zealand Māori culture and were sometimes used for divination. Only the tribal elders knew the spells necessary to make kites fly. Birdman kites have wings, a more or less human-shaped body and a head with hawk or parrot *(kaka)* feathers for hair, shells for eyes and a *moko* (tattoo on the chin).

Jessamine O'Connor

Snowbird

after Mary Noonan's 'In the House'

If I had known, I would have said goodbye years before.

Not at the artificial grass graveside
or the airtight TV room where you all sat like stuffed animals,
but at your table, over the paintbrushes,

or on the coral strand, between sandwiches,
between swims, where I wallowed in the shallows
and admired your distant bobbing head trawling the horizon,

long before the vaporous woman seeped into you,
every year swelling, squeezing more and more out,
until there was only an occasional glint, or a short sharp smile.

There, up the powdery path, against your redbrick wall,
when you unclipped and lifted me from your daughter's bike
and held me high over your face, naming me Snowbird.

It should have been then. If I had known, it would have been then.

Ralph Monday

Blackbird Testament

At dusk the blackbirds sprang up
from the stubble of a van Gogh
wheat field

in unison, primitive force explosion.
A storm cloud of matted ink periods
moving simultaneously in harmony

like a barbershop quartet.
The flock was not broken, knew what
to do without knowing. An ancient

unity possessed them, but it was
the two of us standing in the cold,
watching, that needed exorcism

where we were mute
in the silence spanning years
of slammed doors, broken dishes,

flicker of TVs in separate rooms.
The blackbirds wheeling now like
an angry storm funneled up as an

organic whole,
some dark opal collection, not the broken
thing from which we were seeking respite.

We peered at them
where they vanished like some medieval
spectre at the thin edge of the field.

We knew they understood earth's
magnetic cello sounding out through
the stream of their thoughts, flapping

wings, a text carved against the twilight, a
bitter bible we did not wish to read,
for we tongued the testament.

Eleanor Hooker

Atomy of deceit

A riddle,
it plays soundless games,
soundlessly.
Its crow's feet
tap at nursery doors, its
coarse song a nightmare's lullaby.

It is hush
in the conch shell that
is not the sea,
but which compels
you to press it closer to
your ear, that it may enter.

It is the
eel that eats the eyes
of the drowned,
and being the
temperature
of loss, it is ravenous.

It will climb
the water lily,
suck silence
from its heart.
It is spin, a noxious spew
from Shelob's spinneret.

It tells you
it loves you, its love
is the taste
of sour blue-
clotted milk, sand-suckled blue.
Its love starves every hunger.

It deploys,
will redeploy you
to the stab-lands.
It inks lies
on tattooed cuts of pigskin –
dispatched by money-slaves.

If you say,
yes, take shelter here
beneath my
bound rib-bones,
it will, yes,
and be the death, Nell, for the blackbird
no longer singing there.

Lucid Dreaming

I need to go back in, stay there long
enough to speak to my feathered Shaman;
I need to tell him I was wrong
to be afraid of the mirror Pan,
or the caterwauling from the well.
I check my watch, look away then back
and nine hours have passed; a dream's tell.
In this lucid otherworld the only lack
is colour, the exceptions being my Shaman's
canker eyes, his blond shrivelled wings. My plan
is to find him, describe how my dæmon
takes from my bones the chill of the sea, that began
with the drownings, how he lets me sing truth
to the dark, forgives me the fault-lines of my youth.

Will Stone

Barn Owl

Travelling, you rake
the embers of the rural day.
As the slack ropes of silence tighten
night's giant pike mouth widens, then
the barn owl drops from his hole
to sweep the ghosts of still born lambs
drifting down the lane's black gullet.
He dowses the air, the current is wrong
but he lifts his gaze, secretly sounds
the hunting horn, has his beater the moon
flush out the little ones, the terror-struck,
the thimbles of piping blood
cowering near the shell-hole pool.
There they are rifled by eye, pinioned,
held a moment in a gust of violence,
the straight arrow of supremacy.
Reloaded, he sways on the icy wire,
winkling out shadows, a cinder of amber
from the frost-taut flesh of the fields.

Lia Brooks

Borstal

We sat cross-legged knee to knee.
I was five, the boys grubby and bramble-scratched.
        Carolyn, the eldest,
pointed at you and we looked
up at your scars and holes with the sun
        dropping down behind you. Gnats
billowing below the old elm
like a mass of black eyes, one sometimes
        darting a dark look towards us.

What a giant stumbling over, squatting in the damp
and boarded so your eventide
        spilled through the thin cracks as if blood
through the teeth of a wounded woman.
A permanent evening
        hung thickly inside you,
over the floors of your dusty rooms,
under the ceilings like a sheet you used
        to wrap up the past and hide it with.

I heard an owl. I knew its call
from my mother's cupped hands and cheeks puffing
        some sunny day by a duck pond. And Carolyn
told us about you. Your children lined up in rows,
bed after bed, in the long hall silent and locked out
        from the world.

The boys dared each other to find a way in.
None of us would. It's where
        all the naughty children went.
But if we listened
hard enough, she said, over the owl and elm leaves
        we'd hear them crying in the dark like doors
on old hinges, caught in the wind.

The North in May – *A Suite*

Misplaced

I've turned over shelves,
   there's nothing but paper –

the crimson and green boards
   halved and spineless,

door open on the garden, frost
coming in like kindness

to stay the print of tongue and fingers.
   These letters

commas, exclamation marks,
I have scanned them until tightness

presses above my ears in bands –
a gradual woman seeping

under paragraphs, folding herself
like summer into autumn
and misplaced. How am I to stay

the early hours walking
   room from room? Ice crystallises

the surface of things,
covers my pathways between kitchen

and lounge, first light and evening.
   What a tremendous harm

to be traceless, everything is cold.

*

A Walk

The lining of my coat is sewn with fox fur.

Today, summer won't live along the bank,
the fish grow slower. Low clouds
reflect from their backs, draw inland
against the hills. Trees
move into bud, irresolute.
The hardened sun hangs like a moon,
stags have no expectations – shoots
won't cling white under the soil.

I've taken the longest route
to the loch, lost my way through bracken,
found moss's last green fading
in the cold. The white drifts
flick shadow into silence –
no reason for birds,
no need for the round stomachs of deer.

An alder falls further in.
Its slow thud sends years through branches,
shivering. How cuckoopint caveat
with tight red fists
                      I have come too far

walking into the place quiescence occupies.

*

The Room

Such a fortunate mistake, I was hunting something hole-like and a long way in. I wanted to carry it around, a weather white and frozen to a stone floor. Thin knives of stopped water, clear and pointing from the ceiling. It would be *my* thing. I'd get a jolt, a thrill, sneaking to and from it. It's what all writers want – something consuming to tempt the words out of them... what a fitting mistake. I called and searched until I was found on its intemperate path. And like clay, it was colourless and cold. The touch of it – northern wind, a snowfall on my neck – permanent. A winter to put myself in that I'd neither want nor leave.

*

Clay Hill

I've snuck up upon myself like winter has
on Clay Hill, trees startled bare
against the gaunt distance. The earth is brittle –

mud tracks frozen into peaks and trenches
that collapse under my feet.

I have been unaware of what it is
to be peered into. And like the hole
the owl waits inside, her bowl eyes
full of sap, I can be
nothing but still. Even as I probe inside the gape,

pull out a centipede with my thumb and forefinger.
Even as the wind presses

through the grass. And I am
still pulling out unhatched eggs and bark damp
from autumn's last rainfall
as the wind whirs and drones over feathers,

flicks them up like something immoral
moving within a death.

Paul Murray

On Hearing a Recently Deceased Singer on the Radio

The dead sing pure, purer than the living,
Whenever they sing a song it stays sung,
Their singing is a purer form of giving,
A distillation from an earth-grained lung.
Freed from their grosser selves, their songs are light
They hover in the parted lips of time,
Unanchored as a butterfly in flight,
Ascending scales no living voice can climb.

The dead take nothing with them, nor their song.
They learned from dying not to grasp a world
Of straws, their singing knew it all along.
I sense a sweetness oh so tightly curled
Around about itself like cats at prayer
Circling a fire, no longer even there.

Martin Bennett

Balkan Busker, Metro A, Rome

In some unknown dialect where pain
Must be the norm, as with a chainsaw
He lays into what was once a tune;
Tries, tries, tries, and then tries again,
Self-awarded his umpteenth encore –
Guitar strings at their final tether,
Will-power the stronger for being tone-deaf.
Blues are blues, but here is something other,
Less blues than scratchy relentless greys.
Those wrecked trainers, that half-dyed hair! Head raised,
His eerily coloured eyes conjure a zone
At which safe-salaried commuters shudder
And, to allay more of music's massacre,
They throw as they go a few small coins.

John Gladwell

Zero Gravity

Stay true   to this breath of wind
To this waiting for something to happen
As you then ask   'How far can you take this? How far can you go?'

Learning to live without borders
As once again you ask   'What dreams come with you?
A mosaic of all those years   of lines drawn from your cheeks down to
your chin

With no love to hold us   in this rain   in this night
To close this broken door on your absence   zero gravity
And an indentation on the side of the bed where once we both had lain

Jeffrey Joseph

Intimation

'Josh!' my grandmother cried as they wheeled her
Down sickly, green-smelling corridors,
Where linoleum hushes the route to God knows where
And, brightly solicitous, nurses flutter round trollies
Uttering their worn consolations.

Now, in sleep, my wife's name seems always just at hand,
Ready to be called in desperation
When parting is irrevocable,
When the terror of isolation, actualised like a stone,
Lands on the chest,
And I forget the way to breathe.

Hugh McMillan

The Visitation: Jacob Epstein

She stands
on tip toe,
in a clasp of trees,
hair neatly plaited,
hands folded,
her face pushed forward
into mine as if
I was the voice,
I was the spirit
rehearsing the words
for those straining ears,
'chosen among women'.
But not me,
oh no little Mary,
not me;
remain in stasis,
not speaking, not hearing,
blessed another day.

Gill Learner

Aural History

Grandad's day began with boots on stone, the cage door's
clang. Then the slide down into a perpetual night of axes
picking at a seam, hooves scuffling, trolleys rumbling.
Twice he heard the crack of falling props then yells
and groans. Evenings it was practices for Gala day
with cheering crowds and the four-four of the band.
He strode behind – the heartbeat on the massive drum.

For Aunty Peg it was the hooter, clog-rap on cobbles,
the *ching* of clocking on before mouthed greetings,
nods. Through the thrum of motors and shuttle-ricochet
the girls signed to each other but sometimes, when
a hand was trapped, screams brought sudden quiet.
Saturday night they giggled as they exchanged coats
for cloakroom tickets at the Tivoli and edged into a waltz.

Mum sat one floor up from haberdashery, pressing sums
into a machine. She cranked the handle and a total
chattered onto a paper tongue. Some days she was put
to listen for the clunk of the vacuum tube with a written bill
and cash; she'd count out change and whoosh it down.
At home, dishes washed and racked, she rippled
through piano scales before a Prelude or a Bagatelle.

Dad's fingers made four keyboards rattle and ping,
hammering holes in three-inch tape. The coded reels
made rods and moulds advance, sidestep and retreat
as they beat out characters, line by line, to clatter them into
a page. After supper, rain or dry, he'd quarter the garden
or sit in the greenhouse to a smoke his pipe and talk
to his plants because 'they never answer back'.

What Love can do

A woman dies. Her husband grieves,
commands the quarrying of stone, fine-grained

and whiter than the moon. Many hundred men
carve it into blocks, polish and build them

into a mound, domed and crowned
with an upturned crescent and a lotus bloom.

Craftsmen embed stones – garnet, opal,
amethyst – patterned into flowers and vines

and texts from the *Q'uran*. Here
her bones are locked into a marble tomb

to wait for Shah Jahan.

*

A woman dies; her husband grieves.
Had a doctor's skill been near she would

have lived. But the bulk of a Gehlour hill
spun out the hours. So Dashrath takes hammer,

chisel, nails. For more than twenty years,
ignoring mockery, he snicks the rock

chipping at ancient layers of river silt.
At last, one hundred metres on,

at five times his height and wide enough
for a pair of carts to pass, he's reached his goal –

the mountain's carved in two.

Richard Ormrod

Hands

I no longer
remember
very clearly
your hands:
whether they were
small and delicate
or sensitive
and spatulate
like a pianist's
or watchmaker's;
forty years ago
they were so, so
familiar; so
sought, so known.

Now, alone,
searching the attic
of mislaid memories
amongst the clutter
and detritus of days,
months, years
you never shared,
I can't be sure
any more –
but you penned
an elegant hand
in so many, many
letters I regret
I never kept –

three or four
a day they came
sometimes: full
of hurt rebuke
and accusation –
by comparison
my own were inept.

They were warm
though,
your hands,
I do remember
that: not cold
like pastry-makers,
more like masseuses':
hands that held
me close, then,
finally
pushed me away,
a long yesterday
ago...

David Cooke

Empathy

after Seán Ó Ríordáin

'Come across', said Turnbull, 'you will see such sorrow
    in the horse's eyes.
If you had hooves as heavy beneath you, your eyes too
    would be as sad as these.'

And it was clear to me that he sensed so well the sorrow
    in the horse's eyes
and had thought so deeply on it that his own mind in the end
    had drowned in the horse's.

So I looked at the horse to observe the sadness
    deep down in his eyes,
but all I saw was Turnbull staring back towards me
    from the horse's head.

I glanced at Turnbull, then looked at him again
    until I saw in his face
that the great eyes subdued by sorrow
    had now become the horse's.

Caroline Price

To Iken and back

Walk along the Alde's meanders
from the maltings, leave the concert hall behind
and the sculptures and climb to the thin path
along the dyke: in thirty years
nothing has changed – within minutes
the only sounds are the hush of wind in the rushes
and curlews crying. The duckboards tread over
your past, its creeks and channels
trailing their debris, a strong familiar odour.
Go past the field where you picnicked
to where, below a stand of trees,
the tides have carved that sudden, surprising cove,
a beach hidden from the by-road
where you left the car, dragging the dinghy down
the slope of dark sand: those are the tracks,
still visible, and there a boat still, moored
and shimmering, just out of reach.
The cove is full now, washed with grey
to a perfect scallop, half-submerged.
How important the tides, how delicate
the timing; you have only a couple of hours
to push between withies into the deeper water,
feeling the lurch and uprighting
of the little vessel, hearing the sharp crack
as the sail tautens, fills. Launch yourself
into the river, beyond its troublesome reaches;
forget for a moment how hard the boat is
to manoeuvre, its capsizes, one sister
doubled up laughing as your cousin in a panic
hurls himself upwards and runs
howling along the flattened mast
like a boy running on water . . . This is the place,
and here the upturned peeling hull
that was here then, and the old lime pit;
walk far enough and you will pass the kiln

burning again, the Anchor risen from waste grass
serving the sailors and draymen;
the voices you hear now are theirs, or carry
from the salt works or from Iken church,
alone on its spit, gazing clearly
across reeds to the far side of the river –
Walk back to Iken: you have forgotten
nothing, and it is not sad,
the river narrows and widens again
but everyone you loved is still with you.

Tutu

Darkness still, but the sack was there,
heavy against the bed.
It had burst overnight into flower.
I buried blind hands inside, breathless

yet not surprised – as if I'd seen
my mother's head bent
each evening, determinedly domestic,
over small white stitches, seam after seam

and my father hugging the wayward mass
against him as he crept upstairs
in the early hours, opening the door inch by inch,
heart hammering, terrified,

so that their eldest daughter as dawn broke
could crawl up through the layers
and emerge arms flailing clumsily
into their room, dancing.

Stuart A Paterson

Ebb And Flow

Counting the tides until she gets here,
Some skelping the skerries at Douglas Hall
Like wet hands on dry bodhrans, others
Limping in on a million quiet feet,
And the moons, now here, now gone,
All over the place like a face in circus
Mirrors, I start to count us down as well.
Not by anniversaries or calendared
Occasions but by gaps, passions, yells
Of voiceless conversations under empty
Nets of Solway sky when night was the darkest
Blanket thrown over our happy heads,
Ourselves in the best & messiest of beds.

Fire After Midnight

for Tony Barbour

Long after midnight, we stride through
Wet ferns & chest-high bracken to
Barnhourie Hall, old newspapers in bags,
Thinking of kindling, fire on our minds.
We gather banks of branch, silently
Going about business far older than us for an hour,
Stacking, piling, artfully laying
Stick upon branch upon moss-soft bower.
When the flames take hold & run
Their sizzling length, fireworking tiny geysers
And waterfalls of light up the crumbling lum
And into the dateless sky, it's almost as if
There are ancient oceans lapping the walls,
Millennia stretching unendingly on
To where we'll stride through wet ferns
And bracken, to us, to Barnhourie Hall.

Patricia McCarthy

Not just Coffee Table Books

Anglistik: International Journal of English Studies
  Focus on Literary Illustration (25-1-2014)
Tony Curtis & **David Lilburn**: *Pony* (Occasional Press, 2013, reprint 2014)
  Published in collaboration with Ballynahinch Castle, Connemara
  Copies available from brid@ballynahinch-castle.com
Eavan Boland: *A Poet's Dublin* (Carcanet Press, 2014)

'And what is the use of a book,' thought Alice, 'without pictures or conversation?'
Alice in Wonderland, chapter 1

This quote begins Colin Wilcockson's illuminating introduction to 'Illustrations in Works of Literature', the subject of the ten fascinating essays that demonstrate, through history up to the present day, the varied functions of, and motivation for illustrating, including even comic books, graphic novels and manga genres of illustrations of Shakespeare's texts, in this 2014 issue of the journal *Anglistik*.

Rather than straight illustrations (or mirror images) of texts, it is interesting to note that as far back as medieval prayer books illustrations of narrative material often went beyond the literal text. In his essay on Illustrations to Chaucer's *Canterbury Tales*, Colin Wilcockson tells us that Eric Gill (1882-1940) also went beyond the text, though differently. Gill's lack of reticence in depicting, often in woodcuts, eroticism and sexual scenes, using satyrs which do not feature in Chaucer, show his artwork fulfilling the role of suggestion; the artist here takes the initiative of interpreting the subtext in Chaucer's stories. As well as implying the sexuality inherent in many of them, he goes further and implies 'that sex may lurk subliminally even when the tale is apparently more elevated.' In this way, his artwork adds a kind of visual commentary on the text.

Like many translators of poetry, the illustrator Quentin Blake attempts a 'reflection of the spirit of the text', again subtly commenting on a text by the positioning and repetition of an illustration in order to carry 'an inner meaning' or 'undermeaning'.

Mark Wormald's essay is particularly relevant today, quoting, as he does, Ted Hughes's discussion about the intimate relationship between handwriting and drawing, a relationship which is cancelled out once a computer is used to compose a poem. Hughes favoured an artist such as Baskin who responded to the 'inner nature' of his poetry (Baskin produced the illustrations for *Crow*) which resulted in an inspiring dialogue being established between artist and poet. As Wormald points out, however, Hughes was often worried that illustrations (of drawings or photographs) might become dominant and take over from his poems on the page. A happier collaboration, less threatening to Hughes, was made with the artist Reg Lloyd when each, in turn, would inspire the other. Wormald's recent discussions with some of Hughes's angling friends reveal fresh insights into the creative liaising between writer and illustrator, also its inherent, at times, difficulties and tensions.

As Colin Wilcockson concludes: 'Illustrations often extend the text, without the reader's realisation. There is, in the most successful of author/artist collaborations, a sympathetic engagement so natural that their imaginations fuse into one'.

Carolyn Trant (whose work was on the front cover of the Rilke issue of *Agenda*, for example) would certainly agree with Wilcockson's conclusion. She is a very gifted maker of art books or 'real books'. Hers are inspirational collectors' items housed in major museums and libraries all over the world. She is very enlightening in talking about her work and the encroachment of the digital age. She does art work, often wood blocks, to accompany other poets' work, or her own work. Here are notes she scribbled down for me on a train to the Witches' Museum in Dorset:

> The topography of the material book steers the way I navigate the text, and any images within it; its physical presence can speed me up, or cause me to linger.
>
> I like to feel the heft of how much further I have to go – being told digitally that I have read 67% is just not satisfying. I want a quick glimpse of the shape of the chapters to come, to smell the paper, sense the time passed; savour the type of paper with my fingertips, feel the weight and seriousness of the endeavour, or trip lightly through crackling pages.
>
> The crackle of paper is important – it tells how long the paper was beaten when it was made, the smoothness of its surface hints at 'sizing'; these are technical terms that remind us of the physicality of the world and the labour of making things which enable ideas to be disseminated.
>
> The language derived from how books are made is long embedded in our culture – despite changes from clay tablet to scroll, continuing through the outburst of new papermaking technology in the nineteenth century. It continues in digital formats – we scroll down the screen and yet we still talk about pages; it seems embedded

in our bones that the written culture that has formed us is closely related to the physical form of the book itself.

A screen is insubstantial, a flickering of light – will our new digital consciousness adapt its language? and will it be for the better?

'Flickering' is a nice mercurial word for the speed of thought, but a flicker of light can go out.

I crave the physicality of a text indented on a page (the digital era has seen a great rise of nostalgic enthusiasm for the old craft of hot metal letter press) or its apogee – the feel of the edge of letters carved in stone or wood, words that merit time taken to form, cut and print.

Yes, paper making involves the consumption of a large amount water and raw materials, but used carefully it can be recycled and we should be made to appreciate it more – how much more energy goes towards making a Kindle or electronic device that will soon become obsolete and out of date. A library of Kindles? I don't think so. There is the rapid transfer of basic information; and then there are – books, the result of extraordinary skills and technologies, which can convey thoughts we haven't even thought about yet.

Carolyn Trant's art books are highly specialised and take long in the making, usually wrapped in fine leather covers, with only a few of each kind. No ordinary printers can afford such an endeavour, though Enitharmon did make a fairly close compromise with their 'art books' some time ago.

Perhaps the start of things returning in a full circle, in terms of books versus the screen, is evidenced in less expensive, more carefully-produced, sometimes limited editions that mix art-work or photography, for example, with poems. Even small presses are attempting this such as Mica Press whose *Graphologies* (2014) by Phil Cohen with Jean McNeil is a hybrid text merging the work of a poet/ethnographer and painter that explores, via many genres, the hinterlands of place. Polygon Press, too, with *Wild Adventure* (2014) mixes prose and poetry by Tom Pow in a long poem, accompanied by the delicately detailed artwork of Thomas Watling, the first professional artist in the Australian colony, whose story this collection is about. Five Seasons Press from Hereford also has come up with a very nicely produced hardback book on quality cream recycled paper sourced from scrap generated during printing and converting operations in the UK, with some additions of 'mill broke'. *Lingerings on the Large Day* (2014) by Clive Bush, accompanied by drawings by Allen Fisher, is wide in scope, celebrating England's great scientists, political philosophers, poets and also ordinary men and women. Seventeenth century approaches to medicine link up with the poet's own experience of cancer, all very articulately written.

Pony by Tony Curtis and David Lilburn is an outstandingly fine example of a small press producing an enchanting limited edition. Even the paperback version (there is also a hard copy with an original print included by the artist) is beautiful to hold with its heavy silken paper on which artwork and poems are an integral part of one another.

Tony Curtis's poems, all written with awe, wonder and a tender humour, turn the Connemara ponies that 'appear up out of the earth… like grey misty ghosts' into elemental symbols of our own human nature, an inextricable part of the landscape, the weather and the people in that distinctive part of the West of Ireland. Curtis himself has said of these poems that they are more 'ragged and woolly' than his usual work, and the almost primitive feel of his unadorned style certainly suits the subject.

There are seven ways to know a Connemara pony: by its mane, coat, eyes, hooves, and by its mouth 'That loves to eat words given with pats of the hand', by its nose and by its tail

> That conducts the symphony of birdsong, lake-song, light-song
> That is the bog underfoot, here above the village of Roundstone.

The ponies, most of which are grey, 'the same faithful colour/As Connemara rain', 'Are related to clouds, 'Mist, frost,/Snowflakes and mirrors,//Mirrors and the soft faces of lakes.'

They stand in 'the skinning wind', sometimes 'leap up into the sky',' and are reputed to smell like churches… 'Like the creaky "Star of the Sea"', of 'fairy dust', 'of Guinness, farts and wet grass', and of 'old books, riverbanks,/Bogs, and wool just washed/And hung out in the wind to dry.'

The indigenous people, with their large families, whose lives revolve around the ponies, the pony sales, the pony races, pony shows at Clifden and Maam Cross, the owners, breeders, the sellers who are 'chancers', are characters, with their own wisdoms and senses of humour. Some of them leave more in their wills to the ponies than to their relatives. Sean Halpenny, for example, ignores the poet because '"You called his pony/A horse. That is like calling//A bodhrán/A drum,//A currach/A boat.// It's a wonder he didn't smack you;/I would have."'

The ponies even turn into human characters. In 'Waiting in the Rain', for example, two old ponies remind the poet of 'the two dishevelled characters/In Samuel Beckett's play/ *Waiting for Godot*.' The poem's clever ending echoes lines in the play: the hay man is 'coming soon, very soon,/Perhaps tomorrow.' Other literary references are evident such as the seventeenth century Japanese poet, Po-Nee who preferred herons and ponies to people and who is largely forgotten – a few substantial poems here revolve charmingly around him; Lucian Freud, too, is described painting a pony.

The ponies are also personified: they 'like to read books' on many things including 'On art, poetry, philosophy'; they like Yeats 'and the later/ Paintings of his brother, Jack.'

The poems can be extremely moving. In 'Naming the Ponies', for example, the seven ponies miss Ruth who owned and loved them so much. Old Ned, her widower, 'knows they miss Ruth:/her hands, her voice'.

> She had a way with ponies.
> They like him because they loved her.
>
> The last things she gave him
> Were her names for each of them.
>
> Now, every morning
> In mist, rain or sun,
>
> He calls their names
> Over the gorse like a prayer.

Paintings, sketches and drawings – ink on aluminium, charcoal, chalk monoprints – by David Lilburn sit perfectly side by side the poems and merge into them. There are breathtaking muted but textured landscapes of Connemara, drawings and paintings defined and semi-abstract of the ponies some of which were executed in direct response the poems, others from sketchbooks made over the years.

You don't have to be 'horsey' to appreciate this book; to hold it is to hold the whole of Connemara in your hands.

Place, or perhaps more accurately the spirit of a place, whether lived in or deliberately exiled from, imagined and real, is equally important in A *Poet's Dublin*, published to celebrate the seventieth birthday of Eavan Boland. This special book from Carcanet mixes Boland's best known poems with her own photographs of Dublin. The latter could, perhaps, have been in sharper focus, but they convey beautifully a haunting sense of a Dublin central to Boland's work, a 'double vision' through her artful eye. (Mention must also be made here of the wide-ranging anthology from Dedalus Press, which came out around the same time: *If Ever You Go: A Map of Dublin in Poetry and Song*, edited by Pat Boran and Gerard Smyth, which is a fascinating portrait of a place and its people through time).

Apart from marginalising herself to the suburbs of the city after her marriage, and becoming a self-conscious voice for the woman of the suburbs, (nurturing a wider ambition, it seems, to be the voice of Mother Ireland herself), Boland's poems expand beyond the city's confines into their own universality. The topographical arrangement of the poems, as opposed to a chronological arrangement, enables Boland's work, surprisingly autobiographical at times as she mythologises herself, to be gathered together here like a bouquet to savour, many of the poems like old friends.

Although she might make the bold claim in 'Anna Liffey':

> In the end
> It will not matter
> That I was a woman. I am sure of it.
> The body is a source. Nothing more.

she writes throughout her oeuvre very much as 'a woman', not complying with Virginia Woolf's notion (in her essay 'A Room of One's Own') that there will never be a 'great' woman writer until a woman can write androgynously. Nevertheless, Boland does deserve honouring for being, in her own words, an Irish woman's 'voice'.

An interesting perspective is given on Boland in the long conversation at the end of this book between Boland and Paula Meehan, Ireland's current Professor of Poetry (her new collection will be reviewed in the summer issue of *Agenda*. In fact, I myself, as guest editor then, reviewed an earlier collection of hers in the Irish Poetry double issue of *Agenda*, Vol.33, Nos 3-4, Autumn-Winter 1996). Meehan serves as an interesting contrast to Boland who came from a very privileged background – her family were poverty-stricken in the harsh working districts North of the city.

In this discussion between the two poets, Boland is somewhat repetitive and distant with constant literary references that throw into contrast all the more acutely Meehan's gutsy, lived-in, eclectic perspective as a genuine Dubliner. However, as Meehan wisely observes: 'What I love about poetry is that it makes sectarian or sectional stances redundant.'

Meehan is particularly articulate about the 'cities within cities… all internalised, a kind of inner city within the boundary of the skin'. She adds, 'Aren't we always making the city up? The cities?' She it is should have the last word on the 'dream city': 'It doesn't exactly map on to any known verifiable place. It's the private sonic Dublin each poet makes – the individuated song of the self in place, the free self in the given place. Maybe that's our true city?'

Indeed this could be the 'true city' regardless of name, or even the 'true place' (such as the elemental bog and rocky lands of Connemara) that we all seek inside ourselves, perhaps even communally.

It is heartening to presume, then, that the printed poem should be as safe on the page as on the screen, with or without illustrations, and books, in the future, might have an even better shelf life than now as special editions that will go hand in hand with their Kindle varieties.

Jonathan Barker

'Break the lavender stem, and recorded time'

A C. H. Sisson Reader, edited with an introduction by Charlie Louth and Patrick McGuinness (Fifield Books, Carcanet, 2014)

The book which reintroduced C H Sisson to prominence was Carcanet's *In the Trojan Ditch: Collected Poems and Selected translations* in 1974. Sisson's prose and poetry had already been published by Gaberbocchus, Peter Russell, Faber, Abelard-Schuman and Alan White at Methuen, who published his remarkable novel *Christopher Homm*, told in reverse.

The editors Charlie Louth and Patrick McGuinness, in their scholarly yet also readable introduction, make a good case for his work; in fact probably the most coherent case for his work I have read. They see him as the heir of T E Hulme, although the poetry of Ezra Pound is probably as central – included here is a 1949 review of *The Pisan Cantos* praising lines from the eighty-first Canto as 'magnificent poetry: it is also plain speaking that might serve as a model for any writer, in prose or verse.' And that plain speaking – we find it also in his admiration for Ford Madox Ford – is one of the key elements to Sisson; allied to ideas and allegiances rooted deep in the English history of the 17th century and beyond.

The main part of this book consists of over 150 pages of poems with 300 pages of prose criticism, which mainly consists of essays. None of the early prose fiction is included. More surprisingly there are just eight pages of translations – from Horace & Virgil – mainly reissued from a pamphlet of 1968. Translation is an essential part of Sisson's achievement and the editors admit this is a distortion. But one can see why it would not work to extract parts of Lucretius, Dante or Virgil in a book of already 500 pages. An alternative, in my view, might have been to include a selection from The *Regrets* by Du Bellay – which, in their conversational and simultaneously 'sweet and bitter' tone, are in a way – of all his translations – nearest in tone to Charles Sisson's own way of talking.

Overall, the selection of the poems cannot be faulted. In fact, this selection now may constitute the essential Sisson poems, many of which can be rather lost in the many pages of the 1998 *Collected Poems*. Two poems I missed are the famous Berlin cold war poem 'Over the Wall' dedicated to his friend C J Fox, and the bleak, almost Becketian, poem 'The Corridor' which I can see was probably excluded in terms of length. But I agree with the editors that 'The Discarnation' is one of the central poems, although when I wrote on it in *PN Review 39* in 1984 it was not rated very highly by others. The strict form of the poem focuses the thought and gives us a clear picture of many key Sisson ideas such as his questioning of the importance of the contemporary idea of the individual; our essential nature; our love of place, while maintaining a rather un-Sisson-like upbeat tone throughout .

The poem 'In Flood' is important as it represents a link with Malory's Arthurian stories, also referred to in 'In Insula Avalonia', which is, of course, the historic 'Matter of Britain' central also to the work of David Jones. As this is *Agenda*, it is worth noting that 'In Flood' was a favourite poem of William Cookson and it makes the point that our imaginative and mythic past are also real. 'Burrington Coombe' is an important sequence stressing Sisson's sense of place, where again the realities of the present and the past co-exist, the past informing the present and the present reflecting the past. 'Break the lavender stem, and recorded time' he wrote in 'For Passing the Time'. The poems around the locale of Langport – full of the names of local places – are near in feeling to Ezra Pound's belief that 'What thou lov'st well shall not be reft from thee'. Elsewhere his early and later period poems can appear bleak. For instance, take the memorable early 'The Nature of Man' which views man in an urban environment and concludes: 'but sleep/ Knows us for plants or undiscovered worlds;/If we have reasons, they lie deep.' These lines come from a greater depth than much contemporary verse and show how Sisson was, literally, out of step with his time. 'The poetry owners cannot make me out/Nor I them' he wrote in 'No Address'.

In relation to the critical prose, the editors are also surely right in identifying the *Sevenoaks Essays* – first privately printed as *Essays* in 1967 – as of central importance. Geoffrey Hill included a paragraph as the epigraph to his *Mercian Hymns* of 1971, a book length sequence of prose poem meditations on King Offa of Mercia between 757-796 – 'the presiding genius of the West Midlands' – and wherein, again, the present and the past are contiguous.

The *Sevenoaks Essays* include 'A Possible Anglicanism' and 'An Essay on Identity', both concise expositions on key areas of Sisson's thought. 'It is, indeed, very hard to understand what makes up "I"', the latter begins. Both essays make many profound observations on the life of the 'I' of the individual and the life of the individual in society, with the life of the spirit central to both. The irony apparent to us all – including the editors – is that the 'I' which is so much doubted here is everywhere in evidence in the 'I' of the poems, while a strongly articulate personality is present in every line of the prose essays. The essays on W B Yeats and T S Eliot offer well argued, highly controversial, arguments which run counter to prevailing orthodoxies. Meanwhile the reconsiderations of William Barnes, Edward Thomas and Henry Vaughan remind us of less dominant authentic voices.

The Case of Walter Bagehot, one chapter of which is included here, brings us close to the heart of another aspect of his thought, as in the following extract (not actually the chapter chosen by the editors) where he writes: 'The artist, and indeed the orthodox Christian, cannot fail to find in himself a kinship with primitive peoples, or to regard the accidents of the last few thousand years as making small difference in the essential nature of man'. To Sisson Bagehot believes that 'superior men think wholly in abstractions'. In contrast William Barnes, for example, wrote plainly in language rooted to his actual given world.

Sisson's critical prose shows a strength of emotion linked to a questioning, and often ironically disposed intellect, of which Jonathan Swift was the master. Sisson's mind, in fact, has at root a passionate Swiftian sense of 'savage indignation'. His most logically presented ideas are made vivid by a seriousness of thought and strength of feeling evident on page after page.

W S Milne

Nature's Prism

Pascale Petit: *Fauverie* (Seren, 2014); **Ruth Padel**: *Learning To Make An Oud In Nazareth* (Chatto Poetry, 2014); **Elaine Feinstein**: *Portraits* (Carcanet, 2015); **Mimi Khalvati**: *The Weather Wheel* (Carcanet, 2014)

Les Murray has written of 'the mythic imagination of Pascale Petit' and that imagination continues to be manifested in her latest collection of poems, *Fauverie*. What gives the poems a stamp of personal authority is that she is prepared to take on the tradition in a courageous way. This is clear in the first poem of the volume, 'Arrival of the Electric Eel', which conjures Montale's poem 'L'anguilla', Rilke's 'The Panther' and Sylvia Plath's 'Daddy', an amalgam of primitive emotions akin to the Fauves analogised through a severe concentration on the violence and beauty of the big cats in the Jardin des Plantes zoo in Paris, her 'memory of the dark', she says, vying with her 'appetite for colour'. The talons of the beasts and the burden of words claw at her consciousness equally, realizing the savagery and tenderness of life, its horrifying and ruthless aspects, its daemonic energies, in memories of both her dying father and in the behaviour of the creatures she studies. She feels empathy for the Stone Age cave painters who similarly captured the spirit of animals they hunted, domesticating them through representations in their caves. Those caves are now cages in zoos and private apartments in large cities where chthonic motives and impulses still dominate, where the domineering male still prowls, the 'half beast half father' she writes of in 'Lion Man' (perhaps the most Plath-like poem in the volume).

Incest is the predominant 'appetite' in the volume and a number of poems explore the father's abuse of the daughter in what can only be called a raw fashion (there is no room here for Freudian orthodoxy). I can think of no other poet who has attempted this theme in modern times, in such a personal fashion, and therein lies the courage of the volume: 'goat –/cloven-hoofed father, devil saint'; 'each night she lies like a gutted fish/ for Father the Fishmonger. He strokes her/as if she's a salmon on a bed of ice/that should be dead but is still twitching'.

> My father crept into the storeroom –
> right up to my camp-bed.

> He closed the door so gently
> even the spider didn't hear.
>
> He took out a handkerchief
> and whispered that darkness
>
> was wrapped up inside it,
> passed it over my face'...
>
>   (from 'Lord of the Night')

There is more of this sort of thing, and it is very disturbing like the gargoyle-spook that sits on the private parts of the sleeping woman in Henry Fuseli's painting, *The Nightmare* (1781) or the creepy physician who leers over a woman's corpse in Gabriel von Max's *Der Anatom* (1869) but less posed, less literary, more real. This is a world away from the child-brides of Petrarch, Dante and Edgar Allan Poe, for instance. The nocturnal visitations of the father are likened to the hot breath of the big cats in the zoo – the lions, the leopards, the jaguars.

Elsewhere in the volume the poet's gourmandising father (he is a louring, threatening presence throughout the volume) is seen relishing an ortolan which has been force-fed with maize and drowned in a vat of Armagnac before being sizzled for eight minutes in the pan (surely the cruellest food in France, though she also writes of the gavage of foie gras – readers may like to know it is reported ortolan was on the menu of President Mitterand's last meal, along with foie gras, a capon and a bottle of Sauternes). The cruelty of appetite (Petit writes of 'my face pierced by jaguar whiskers', and later, in another poem, she provides us with the word's etymology, '*Yaguará* – meaning/he – who – kills –/with – one – bound') is stressed throughout the book, in all its carnal avatars. None of this makes the poet feel any better. She tells us 'Her tongue is like a soiled mattress' describing these brutal activities ('the dangerous/ work of the mind... confronted in animal form').

Towards the end of the book she discovers some kind of forgiveness in nursing her dying father, but somehow the relentless brutality of the preceding poems dominates as the overriding tone. *Fauverie* is a disturbing book with a stamp of personal authority which one rarely hears in contemporary poetry. It is a work which makes us nervous, shaking up our sensibilities, upsetting our mental and moral schemes.

If in *Fauverie* we encounter a strong female personality dealing courageously with the violence of patriarchy in a largely domestic setting (though she is concerned also with the question of the extinction of species), in Ruth Padel's *Learning To Make An Oud In Nazareth* we meet a private individual engaging with the public violence of the Middle East, trying to make sense of the clash of cultures ('the task/is to assimilate, to move between the languages' she writes, 'to translate old words into new', 'translating human earth/to the abstract and divine'). Her poetry interleaves passages from *The Song of Solomon* and the *Psalms* ('fore-memory of blood') with contemporary apprehensions and images ('as lustrous as under-leaves of olives beside the sea'), limning the continuity of struggle, the rise and fall of empires. In a poem on The Crucifixion it is evident she is not trying to impress by force but is, in fact, frightened of it, as she dwells on Christ's dying, fearful hours, as his spiritual being is torn apart by opposing political powers. The tone of Padel's poems is polite and civilised, pitching against the extremity of the times. She believes in sanity, in balance, in conveying the suffering and affliction of the region, but placing these qualities and issues in a wider historical context (she writes of Homer's 'clear-voiced lyre' for instance, and of Euripides' 'scalpel pity and songs'). She writes of 'David's harp', Herod, Judas, Constantine, Justinian, Jerome, the Crusades, Schindler, and so on, ensuring her verse remains within a public arena:

> We identify. Some chasm through the centre
> must be in and of us all: creatures of relation
> and division, always wrong-footed by the past
> on its bed of ice , the sub-tectonic clash
> of ancient histories on common ground.

Ruth Padel's poetry deepens our sense of reality, and widens our historical imagination. If at times one feels that Petit surrenders to the nightmare of nature, in Padel we feel not only does she not honour the chthonic (Emily Dickinson's the seed 'that wrestles in the Ground'), but she does her utmost to fight against any temptation to yield to it. A phrase of Camille Paglia comes to mind when contrasting these two poets: 'There is... nothing beautiful in nature. Nature is primal power, coarse and turbulent. Beauty is our weapon against nature; by it we make objects, giving them limit, symmetry, proportion. Beauty halts and freezes the melting flux of nature' (in *Sexual Personae,* 1990). Petit is drawn to the amoral chaos; Padel is not. She states clearly enough: 'What would we be without desire for form?/ Pattern keeps us safe... Making is our defence against the dark'.

The title of Elaine Feinstein's latest book, *Portraits*, is self-explanatory. The poet presents us with sketches of writers and artists whom she has known or imagined, including Martina Tsvetaeva, Anna Akhmatova, Isaac Rosenberg, Jean Rhys, Sylvia Plath, Enzensberger, Joseph Roth, Wisława Szymborska, Disraeli, Joseph Roth, Zelda Fitzgerald, Siegfried Sassoon,

Billie Holiday, Bessie Smith, and Edith Piaf. She is concerned with finding what is best in their work to pitch it against what she sees as a dearth in the contemporary world:

> Although in Delphi there is no oracle,
>   no cave of murmurs,
> in the ruins of Apollo's temple,
>   behind broken columns...
> The god himself has vanished
>   as if no-one ever brought
> goats and treasure into his sanctuary
>   to beg his healing power.

At times she is even doubtful of the efficacy of the finest art, asking 'But what does any poet know deeply enough,/other than an inner world of shadows?', as if all existence were solipsistic. Yet her own poetry belies this apprehension, instantiating energy, intuition, instinct, sensual capability and imaginative vision:

> We are halfway through the dark time.
>   They know it in their roots, the winter trees:
> while I sit brooding over the keys,
>
> out here in the garden, snow coming on,
>   they need no plan to blossom and seed –
> the earth provides for their time to come.
>
> If words could rise as simply, I should sing
>   of the power – never to be proved or shaken –
> whose silence answers human aspiration.

Poetry is our shadow, and knowing this, Feinstein quotes Akhmatova as saying, 'Our shadows live for ever'. Here we have a poetry of luminous images, restoring the sharpness of sensory experience and memory, a private voice (like that of many of her 'portraits') resisting the dictates of authoritarianism.

Like Marianne Moore, Mimi Khalvati gives us intimate poems on the lives of the smallest creatures – the house mouse, the mouse lemur, the sun sparrow, the snail, the eastern grey squirrel, and the bat. For her, nature does not appear so mysterious, so cruel and blatantly aggressive as it does to Pascale Petit. It is not quite so miasmic or formless (each poem is sixteen lines long, set in couplets, Khalvati playing variations throughout the sequence). She is more certain of her footing: 'We grow older, quieter,/ hearing degrees of movement, distance, and the dead//would listen if they could to the voices of the living/as bedrock listens to the ocean'. We are far from Medusa's hissing serpent-hair, or the Dionysiac revels of *Fauverie*. Although the poet is open to the experiences of place and history (we have a number of poems on London, the Mediterranean, the Canaries) the form of her poems remains compact and tight, never wandering from the bright image and the luminous insight ('umbrellas of light', 'golden stars of hamlets', 'rain in massive drifts', 'a silence that rings in the ears'). The critic Helen Vendler has written that many contemporary poems 'are coming to resemble cloud chambers full of colliding protons rather than a well-wrought urn' (in an essay on the poetry of Adrienne Rich and Jorie Graham, collected in her book *Soul Says: On Recent Poetry*, 1995) and I think it is this tendency that Khalvati is resisting in her sequence of poems, attempting to find hope and meaning in the seeming formlessness of nature. This quality (borrowing a phrase from H.D.) she calls 'The Overmind', that part of consciousness which pitches art against nature: ' It was the permisson and palm side by side // like two wise prophets and the view that dipped / then rose, the swallows that turned the valley. // It was the machinery of the old olive press, / the silences and the voices in them calling'.

Whether writing on animal or human life, or evoking rich landscapes, Mimi Khalvati never loses her eye for lyrical detail. Particularly touching are the poems on the death of her mother, and how she deals with her grief:

> Let them be, the battles you fought in silence.
> Bury your shame, the worst you thought in silence.
>
> At last my beloved has haggled with death.
> 'One more day' was the pearl she bought in silence.
>
> At night she heard the blacksmith hammering chains,
> at dawn the saw, the fretwork wrought in silence.
>
> 'The only wrong I've done is to live too long',
> my beloved's eyes tell the court in silence...

The tone of the book is never impatient or anxious. The poet shows none of that self-pity, self-centredness or self-chastisement we too often encounter in contemporary 'confessional' poetry. Khalvati's writing is acute, observant, reflective and formal – *The Weather Wheel* is a memorable book.

Tony Curtis

Two Poems

i.m. Elizabeth Bishop 1911-79

House

You wondered how I got the house
In North Haven, Maine.
Well, I saw it in the newspaper.
Wooden, faded cedar,
Lonely as my grandmother's house.

I called the number. A woman's voice
Asked, 'And what do you do?'
In case she didn't trust poets or poetry,
I replied, 'I like to paint a bit and watch
The sandpipers running on the wet sand.'

'As long as you're neat, and there are
No dogs or men involved, you'll do.'
'I'm allergic,' I said, 'neat as a seamstress.'
'You're a poet, aren't you?' she said,
'Come now! The sandpipers are waiting.'

Self-portrait Nude with Lota

If she had been born a boy, she said,
She would have been a rough sailor.
But she was born a girl and grew up
A drunk who drank with disappointed sailors.

If she had been born a bird, she said,
She would have been a shy sandpiper
Chasing the waves in and out all day,
Not a care in the world but the weight of water.

And yes, if she could have been born an animal,
She said, she would have been the moose
That came out *of the impenetrable wood,*
Stood on the country road and stopped her bus.

And if she could have been born a place,
She said, she would have been a sheltered bay
With a fisherman's hut and a red boat bobbing,
Or an island with a smouldering volcano at its heart.

But the story goes she lost Everything!
Starting with her father, then her mother,
Then her mother's mother and her mother's father,
Then her mother's sister, then her uncle...

One by one until everyone was gone,
Even her lovers, the casual, the precious.
Even the old loved house in Nova Scotia.
Then she herself fell away, poem by poem,
                              She was autumnal.

Do you know she painted watercolours?

A tall wooden house in Key West;
The porthole in her cabin; a crumpled hotel room
In Paris, all higgledy-piggledy, the air
Thick with cigarette smoke and longing.

Having read her poems and her letters,
Having looked at her frail little drawings,
I imagine somewhere there is a watercolour
Called *Self-portrait Nude with Lota*.

In it Elizabeth is bending over Lota
As she shampoos her lover's long black hair.
Across the valley the forest bush
Is darkening and darkening.

It is probably kept in a drawer
Out of the Brazilian light.
Occasionally someone looks at it
And wonders who these naked women are.

Or perhaps, now that I think on it
More than likely, she burnt it,
Her life, like her past,
Gone up in flames.

Mario Petrucci

Frau Beckmann

(Berlin, December 1943)

Max, I have tried to understand your letters.
Franz is asking for you, for the pen. Your dark
eyes are his. Why won't you lay my mind to rest?
What is this putting Mona Lisas in crates?
Meeting with priests instead of your officers
while they make of Germany's best blood a lake.
Today an officer came, called you 'meddler'.
Mentioned the eastern front as he ate your cakes.
You careless man! What? Have you turned Britisher?
You know what they can do, Maximilian.
Have you forgotten your Yiddish half-mother?
What are abbeys to me? Is art our concern?
Do your duty. Now. By the book. I expect
an assurance. Next post. You want to see your son?

David Ball

In the Hotel Negresco

The rich are different from you and me.
Yes I know, don't tell me, they have more money.
Isn't that what I was saying? And what I wanted
to go on to say was that that makes a difference:
that when you're born rich, when all your life
you can buy whatever you want, or have it
bought for you, you don't even have to rely on
your own taste, you can pay for everything,
anything and everything, and on top of that,
everyone you know is just as wealthy, then
doesn't that make a difference?

They're raising their voices, that group over there,
the couple in the middle, shouting in English…
Watch out, she's climbing on to the table!
She's dancing! She's kicking the ashtrays on to
the floor. That's her husband, I guess, clutching
his drink…
I have to practise! I'm in love with Madame.
I have to please her. She believes in me.
She tells me that it's not too late.

Rococo colours of pink, powder blue and pale yellow,
a roof of partly coloured glass letting fall over a vast space
a discreet, distinguished light, over portraits of monarchs
sumptuously attired – all yours for the day,
nostalgia included at no extra charge.

David Pollard

The Dark Fiddler

i.m. Frederick Delius

Back again
into the ever glad and dancing
sun's dark love among the oranges;
again to ride the rivers of our lust
in recollection
and to find
my little sad mulatto of recall
lost in the grasses' low and level
wasteland now devoured
by too rich harmonies of horn
bassoon, flute, strings,
their chordal lush
backing away
into the orchestration of my life's
chromatics that refuse themselves
for other exiles before Frederick,
to Fritz, Fritz, Fritz.

Back
from the patriarchal whip
that never heard a note
and back
beyond the gay and flaunting
Parisian decade of the dead
and from my no arms syphilitic
blind and unbodied lameness
to the notation, black with a silence
broken by the pen into its own
and other almost recollections.

Back I went to find my youth in yours
and found only the emptiness
of loss and exile of my art
always the colour of that first love
and the high sparrow calling of my youth.

Britten

Twelve tone's a language
I cannot make meaning out of,
speaking as I do a kind of past
tonality of death's republic.
Thus I withdraw with Mstislav
and the cello suites and other
parables that speak of all those early
deaths I walk with at my own pace.

So Berio and his ilk can stride
before me into the catastrophic
branches of the modern
while I under another sun
to death in Venice where
Aschenbach (invisible worm)
and Wagner
on the sickening waters'
lap against the last quartet
and bells and bells ring out
above the river of the mind's
own secret life
pungent with its alleys and tides,
its bodies plagued with dreams
         to
serenissima
and, if the notes allow,
         beyond.

Roland John

Bombed Out

It was the era of studio, portrait photography,
my glamorous aunt, peroxide blonde, has her place,
but it is my father, whom I hardly knew that stares down
in black and white. An officer, a gentleman I presume,
comfortable in his RAF blue, the crown and wings
on the jaunty angle of his cap, that cautious smile.

From such relicts and half-remembered tales
we construct a simulacrum of possibilities,
events that may have happened, desperate
to pin down the commonplace, to make
a display from fragments and homely lies,
these and haphazard snapshots are all I have.

I have few real memories, flying kept him away,
my mother told me little, I assume they had
the usual problems brought on by absence,
temptation, war. We lived more comfortably
than most, a productive garden supplying needs –
my grandmother's house – the piano's silver frames.

Angela Croft

Waving

Long after the War my brother
was posted to Jamaica,
danced with the girls to a calypso band,
until he was laid low with prickly heat,
brought me back a towel flushed
with hibiscus and a small enamelled ring
he'd found washed up in the sand,
slipped from a child's finger
into the cerulean sea, while I shivered
in waves of liquid metal, savoured
the salt, imagined her dart like a fish
through a current more powerful
than the wind, drew warmth
from her sunripe island, where she waved
back at me, her new flag, with its gold
saltire fluttering like a yellow bird
that never touches the ground.

Caroline Smith

Mr Giang

veteran of the American war

Smoke stains the lining of his nose.
He listens to the chime and chink
of riddled barbeque coals
that hover flames
sweeping jagged
when a squirt of lighter fuel
drapes across them.
He watches the casual ease of his grandson
twirling over his knuckle
a cloth of purple flopping meat
as he nonchalantly adjusts the grill
talks animatedly to the guests.

A baseball mitt of steak
is plumped down on his plate,
a pool of red rain collected
in the patchwork leather.
Grandpa Giang speaks sixty-two
Vietnamese bird languages,
but in his eighteen years in America
he hasn't yet mastered English.
He concentrates on the words
but as he stretches out to grasp them
they squawk out of reach
disappearing into the haze of mist
that hangs dripping over the rainforest canopy
where the noise of bird song
is louder than a city.

The echolalia of foreign sounds
stutter stubbornly in his throat,
catching on stumps of charred,
defoliated forest
that emit only the ghostly
calling of the gibbons
and the breathless whistles of the birds.

Dan MacIsaac

Torrington

He was the first man downed,
the head stoker
lugged from the *Terror*
like a sack of steam coal.

Hunchbacked into a hole,
his small coffin, shrouded
in filthy cloth, was cached
under frozen ground.

Lead from boiler water
or tins soldered
by the lowest bidder
had clogged his blood.

His stunted bones
lay like pipe
in the pine box.

His flesh meagre
as melted wax,
floated pale as floes.

Torque of ice-worms
wrenched, bursting
his black lungs.

Head haloed
with frost,
jaw slung shut,

his eyes glared
against the profanity
of light.

Note: John Torrington, a member of Franklin's ill-fated Third Arctic Expedition of 1845-6, was the first to die in that mass disaster. In 1984, a team of scientists exhumed the stoker's frozen corpse. The autopsy revealed a body poisoned by lead and ravaged by emphysema, pneumonia and TB.

Sue Mackrell

Singing Their Way to the Ancestors

Listen to the wind-howl on stormy seas,
shrieking in the rigging, voices of the dead,
drowned, damaged cargo
jettisoned, tossed to sharks eager for rich pickings,
feasting on red gobbets of flesh, a body dismembered,
bone, cartilage, vertebrae snapped apart,
a line of bones on the sea-bed mapping
oceans divided by compass, tracking triangular
way marks of slave routes,
a skull picked white, threaded by sea-worms,
a wrist-bone, skeletal hand, iron chain embedded in bone.

A cacophony of vengeance hangs in the air,
incantations echoing,
a wailing lament, keening,
an ululation of anguish
for the dead, for the unborn,
for those who will never be born
and whose souls will not travel
the spirit path to the lands
of the ancestors,
to be buried in red soil or dark clay,
in ancient tribal lands beneath the boundaries
of empire imposed territory,
interred in rock-caves,
cremated ashes in a bone-urn
to be revered, respected by those who follow.

Souls of Ewe, Ibo, Ashanti,
Mandingo, Feti, Foulah
still singing their way home,
Yoruba calling down the storm god, Shango,
rolling drums of thunder,
a forked flash of lightning,
Eshu the trickster god wreaking retribution,
tormenting the torturers,
haunting stories told by sailors
of strange sounds, a scream ripping apart the skies,
a howling, roaring, warning.

Note:
Captains of slave ships threw men, women and children overboard if they could get more money on insurance than the slaves were worth alive. The 1890 Brussels Act was the first comprehensive anti-slavery treaty which allowed the inspection of ships and the arrest of anyone transporting slaves.

Bred in the Bone

Bred in the bone of South Wales valleys,
she made good, married, moved to London.
But she wanted the warmth of stone and brick terraces,
smell of wet slate hanging in the air,
mingling with the acrid tang of coal dust,
rain falling between stone walls,
the round scullery window
framing bluebells on the mountain
massing blueness on green,
and red tulips in the blackened cinders of sparse soil.

On holidays I was paraded
in hand-made dresses, smocked and shirred,
pinking sheared seams lovingly stitched
on the prized Singer sewing machine,
shiny black with gold lettering.
She lost her city 'nerves' here,
let go enough that I had her childhood's freedom
to play near the river running black with coal dust
and slide down pre-Aberfan slag heaps,
hard shards of clinker sharp under my Clark's shoes,
clinging to the mountain ash trees
berry bright against the black,
tenacious in the gritty dirt.

She died young, should have been buried in the valley
but instead was scattered in a south London cemetery.
And I wore a black dress she hadn't made.

Howard Wright

The Gritter

The bevelled gritter is behind us, then before us,
blocking our view, and making for the lower ground.
The angled monster cuts in and bestows grip
to the carrion road. We enter safely through a fantail

of gravel and stinging salt pelting, flying
off the chassis... Buckshot, sand in the eye,
gabstones of hell along the gut of the camber
blazing a trail over killer hills dark as feathers.

Marina

Once-plush functionalism fails to heal beneath a reticule
of scaffolding, flush windows
legally flaunt triangular sails
with a view over the marina, daughters' names, goddesses,
hulls and masts and lines all angled, strained and neat,
the listing 'Shearwater' taking the spooned silt
like medicine from the precariously nimble JCB...

God is in the details, but details can be changed:
the wrong colour of pink; bawdy gnomes; a lough
slipping under morning mist high and mighty and as white
as a cross-channel ferry...

Buildings, cranes, boats, planes erased; no seagulls,
no traffic to count, and the hills, once brutal, stubborn, plain,
suddenly beautiful. Without the city, this place
is now our own. Not a sound. Run them by me again:
Marshal Ney. Curacao. Vienna...

Omar Sabbagh

Fathers

For the Haddad Family

I know my father. They know theirs.
And between the winking of an eye
Each father declares
Steel missions of rubble and aching,
Feeling the ticks of rising Time,
Sun-splendour, and sovereign rhyme –

Father, to you, I commend this song
Of words beyond the briefs of sundry signs…

And your sleeping agony's mine because
The forestry of your lap once greenly was
My body's prop, my small, my final cause –

Arenas of four burly oaken doors
Striding into the future

And that life that farther life adores.

Julie-ann Rowell

Rocking Horse

We were discussing things finished with, gone,
as we studied her rocking horse in the shop window
– *eighteen hundred bucks* –
a bargain for fifty years of memories
from her dead father's apartment
on Seventy-Third, the horse motionless now
with its little red saddle and charcoal mane,
never one for running away.

We left it behind in an East Village drizzle
as my friend mourned other losses –
the chequered taxi with its roomy inside,
the driver who'd take you anywhere
while today no one knows the back streets
of Brooklyn, or that sushi bar in Queens
where she took her lover in the seventies.
The rocking horse had stayed the same, she said

with its chequered grin and ride to nowhere.
At times it stands four square, dappled grey,
in her dreams, snorting at blocks
around which her dead father totters still.
Counting out the dollars, eight hundred, ten…
I saw she'd said goodbye to that certain past,
her father, and all that stuff besides.
And I didn't need to buy her childhood back.

Noel King

Timoleague Fete

We cast dice for an Easter cake to carry home; prize booty,
but a fat boy from the village wins it. We watch him
stuff an unwashed finger into it and fill his chops.

In the shooting gallery we can't even get a Roosevelt –
as they call the soft little toy bears – for the baby at home.
We don't dice for any more fare, spend on candyfloss

till our money's gone and there's only the one tuppence-ha'penny
between the lot of us. Father won't mind we're skint
as tomorrow is Good Friday, there'll be church and that.

Mother makes Christmas cakes but never Easter cakes.
At Easter you get a *guggo* – a plain egg with a melted sugar
coat you suck off. Then with a pin slit at the end

you suck out the yokes and white; string thread through the egg,
make a dream catcher thingie on a wire coat hanger.
Mother hangs it over the television to keep evil away.

Robyn Rowland

Garavogue Session

for James Carty and Francis Gaffney

James leans back languid beside long riverside windows
after a late-night early-morning session in the Snug
packed too close. Flute, hovering, barely touches his mouth,
skin only moist with its soft imprint, all sweetness in the breath,
and plays a slow air drawn across morning like honey
dropping slow, amber and resonant as memory.

Reluctant at first, Francis fingers strings light as raindrops
falling carefully on the dipped backs of swans on the river.
Garavogue, An Gharbhóg, 'rough youth', it is swift today
twirling with white water on the cascades then whirling
up-river briefly before sweeping across and along the rocks.
It risks tripping, speed being the careless swing of the young.

The flute is riding now, waves of it surfing, sweeping sure
and slowly easing into the bank where swans should be
sleeping in still water if spinning were not the
motion of this morning. Now breath moves into a jig,
suddenly as the player takes up the day riding the rise into
lightness and back waves spiralling under a sudden surge.

The river rushes. Guitar holds the tune above water.
Then his voice grows around a song, holds the *n* and *m*
compressed at the back of the throat in the old way. He sings of
love enduring from the tops of mountains, of the grace of swans
and women. And though it weaves through the mist of myth
the nightingale, tireless in the beauty of these unwounded gifts.

Terry McDonagh

On the Train to Dublin, July 1st 2014

To my late mother on her birthday and i.m. Dermot Healy

The sun has microfilmed – there's no need for tears.
My mother and Dermot Healy are dead. They never

met and died seven years apart but dead is dead as this
perfect day rises in me. I'm not in a tall building, but,

at least, I'm travelling first class by default. A mother
teaches her little son to be best in his class. I feel like

shouting: stop colouring in that ugly horse – there are
three beauties out there in the meadow. Should I report

this woman for stifling vim and vigour – for
damage to a boy's head – for anti-social behaviour.

They are a unit contracted to each other. The boy
knows how to spell house and roof and suburbia.

He's learning to keep the lid on things – to cover up.
A completed construction might read: the roof is there

to keep you safe – under lock and key – out of
danger – out of harm's way – I'm your mother.

Your mother means well.
She is indebted to you.

Jesus, Mary and Joseph meant well
in paradise.

Allah meant well
in paradise.

Dermot Healy meant well – Dermot Healy did good.
He watched birds migrating.

My mother meant well – my mother did good.
She watched me migrating.

Look out of the window, boy. Stop colouring in
for a moment. Look at those horses taking wing.

Imagine the moon ducking among the stars. Imagine
the dead catching up on games they'd forgotten

and, above all, don't forget
to build a skylight into your roof.

Kate Hendry

Moving On

For months, since I moved to this city,
I've imagined bumping into you,
sure I'll catch you on a weekend
at hers, parking up your rusty Fiat,
fishing out the keys she gave you.
Today, awkwardly, I stand on her steps,
number 33, St Stephens Lane,
her glossy railings and white front door.

On my first visit, years ago, I paused
on the stairwell, looked up,
past iron banisters, and saw you
and your new woman, peering down.
You'd invited me to her one-bed flat
to see the wooden floor you'd helped her lay.

I check the names on buzzers.
Campbell, Martin, Mitchell, Brown.
I read them all. She's sold up
and I realise – as when I saw
her double bed and your blue jumper,
the one I gave you, the one you shrank,
lying on her duvet next to her scarf –
that you're gone, for good.

Dreaming You Want Me Back

It's one of those dreams – you finally realise
you love me and shouldn't have let me go.
Your other life hasn't worked out.

I'm inside your narrow boat.
I forget you might be dangerous,
like the risks of smoking to my heart.

I've come back to remonstrate
and I've got to see it through.
You've offered me a second-hand marriage –

watching the news with tea on trays,
washing up left till morning,
going to bed at different times.

It's a deal I can't help wanting –
to be sitting in bed with you, our bed,
looking at the black sky through the hatch.

To stop myself I talk too fast, too loud.
I wag my finger and tell you in a pompous tone
that's not what love is about.

Gill McEvoy

Where Are the Men?

Too many mothers stitching and snipping
their fine, fine clothes, patting their shoulders,
smoothing the folds.

How these priests glow in their greens and their golds,
dazzle and sway in their whites clean as moons.

They mutter by gravesides and sorrow's dark bed,
carrion crows in their deadly black robes,
are led away then by the mothers, and fed.

One of the mothers, withered and grey
sweeps out the priest-cave, stands guard at its door,
breathes fire on petitioners, sends them away.

Deep in their hearts are they really small boys
playing at dressing up, messing with toys,

the mothers all sighing,
isn't he handsome, isn't he fine? –

Oh, too many widows who burn with desire
and secret designs to play round with fire.

CHOSEN BROADSHEET POETS

Françoise Harvey, 32, writes poetry and short stories and has been published in *Bare Fiction Magazine* and in the For Books' Sake anthology *Furies*. Having grown up on the Isle of Man, she now lives in London and finds that her background in Manx culture, particularly the music, is currently informing a lot of her work.

My love plays the fiddle on Southbank

Take your missteps along the Southbank and find her.
Dodge the crowded flow and follow the floating notes.

Let them wind around your wrists and ankles. Welcome their grip.
Let them wend, hot in your ear, skimming your skin
a thrill air of noise that calls you past still trees and benches.

Dance you, puppet, to the spot where she plays –
knee bending on the one, waist dipping to the three.
She snags your eye and gifts you a nod.

I know. Your heart'd beat as fast as her fingers, wouldn't it?
That pluck and bounce and a tap up the long neck
so high by the varnished curve and then, tease, bowing low and slow.

Watch her caress the strings back to tune
stretch the waves longer, snap them to a spiking height.

Hold your breath.

She raises the slim stick and

drops horse hair to catgut, swoops to the right, galloping, balancing,
arpeggios falling
scaling the rise, jump to a jig, fingers twitching, toes tip-tap.
Remember when we used to play?
DrowsyMaggieMasonsApronLarkintheMorningWindshakestheBarley
oh god, that one, that step, you know
that glissando, the tremolo and double-stop and hop across to

RockyRoadRattlinBogWildRoverEunyssaghVona
play bodhrán on your forearm with a plastic fro-yo spoon.
She builds to allegro – the rush of it! – slides to largo – a drawling flow
fades out to the end with a cross-string sigh and you there

take a breath of the cleared air and whistle the long walk home.

At Canada Water

Under the slump of a steel-sky day,
out on the white-noise water,
the moorhens are loving and reeds are a-sway
with the careless destruction of weather at play.

Racing, wrestling, over the water
the crosswinds kiss and run away.
A gull is drop-diving and hot for the slaughter
of fishes and bodies the waves have brought her.

Artless eyes should look away
or learn loving on the water.
Ducks swim together and on the pagoda they
romance and flirt: soft, feathered foreplay
under the slump of a steel-sky day,
out on the white-noise water.

Life finds a way

Are you there, clusterling? Aren't you?
Brave one, you are a determined would-be,
catching and growing in these hostile waters.

We set nets to trap your beginnings, kick-foot.
I warned you off with silver, took potions,
sometimes leant on the power of prayer.

Are you there?

Each moon you're a threat and maybe until
the redded rag waves the war won and you gone,
lost in a churning of not-nows and could-have-beens.

On the tide, move on and up. Ride out the swell.
Hide safe in the deepest and darkest where
you swiften, sing and fly.

The Understudy

(after Ravel's Piano Concerto for the Left Hand)

Sinister, the rise and swoop is calling memory.
The stuttered beat prompts the thrum of a ghosting pulse;
gut hails bone to bear the arm's shorted weight.

Shaded fingers press silently and dream still to stone
as the clumsy forgotten lifts and fans, pops gristle,
shakes shackles, forgets its place.

Understudy, take the lead and take the piece!
All the fluttering speed of the possessed –
such storming flight is the right of one left behind.

Slide south to a triumph and pause;
catch the fullness, the high to the low.

They dance, they dance, the five set free.

Jon Bridge, 35, is an academic scientist and writer living and working in Sheffield and Liverpool. His wife and two children occupy most of his thinking time outside of work, and if he could choose one place to do that thinking it would be on a wide, blowing beach in the west of Ireland.

On Carrownisky

i (A stranding)

Wet sand strafed
by cloud-wracked
sun-light amplifies
and recombines until
the bomb-bright
million-sun light
bares your atoms
silhouettes your heart
imprints the structure
of your self
upon the strandline,
absolute eternal now.

ii (Return)

Soft rain falls faintly
upwards from the mirrored
sand-swash.

Dancing there above a
realised shadow-you,
wind-glowing, hair blown
back a hundred or a thousand years,

the shining strand stretched thinly
brings about a transubstantiation
here, beneath a sudden crown
of lightening sky, the vaulting blue

reflected, punctured now and then
by foam; an absolution, priest-less,
welcoming a child home.

iii (The midden)

They light a fire on the strand each year – more often if they can –
and mark the passing time in nameless ceremony.

Rituals evolve: construction of the fire pit from sand;
who makes the Thermos tea; who keeps the twist of butter for the pan.

The celebrants change gradually as well. The year-marks one can see,
the lifelines lengthen on the hands. Eyes deepen. Children's names
change.

And all around the dunes shift silently remembering
the warmth of bodies gathered round a flame, the

heat and light sustaining down the generations, much the same.

Luke Palmer, 30, lives and works in Wiltshire. He writes poems, some of which have been published.

Two Births

       i

Slipped out. Clay
gulped onto the hillside
in bone china silence.
Trussed in its own birth cyst

eyes glued shut and
mulched in milk-thick steam
it looked nothing like the lamb
it should have been.

From this distance, more like
a cloud shot down;
a slice of moon;
an egg sack.

We squinted through rain
for signs of movement,
thinking of small rooms,
nooks, the spaces in between.

Turned towards home
passing barbed wire
along the cliff edge
we leaned over.

Enough nook for all of us
down there.

ii

Gripping black fleece
I felt the strength of the ululations
as moons stirred within her
pulling the brine tide along

and out onto soft grass.
A snout. A snout and two hooves
came first then
stopped.

Thick hands grasped
and out it shuddered.
A slick wave washed
onto the deck of the field

a deep sea creature,
useless gills reaching
at something
or digging.

Fingers pierced
the convex gasp
of the amnion.
Damp lungs fluttered.

I let go.

NOTES FOR BROADSHEET POETS

Interview with Kathryn Maris by Simon Collings

Kathryn Maris, a poet from New York who has lived in London since 1999, is the author of *God Loves You* (Seren, 2013) and *The Book of Jobs* (Four Way Books, 2006). Her poems have appeared in *Granta*, *Poetry Review*, *Ploughshares*, *Poetry London, Slate*, *Poetry*, *The Spectator* and *The Financial Times*, as well as in many anthologies, including *Best British Poetry* and *The Pushcart Prize Anthology*. She teaches at the Poetry School in London.

Kathryn, you're an American poet living in London, someone influenced by both US and British poetry traditions. We'll talk about the two cultures and the trends you observe in contemporary poetry, but let's start with your early influences. You grew up in New York and attended school there. Who first got you interested in writing poetry?

I started writing from a very early age without many models except Dr Seuss and children's poetry. But the first poem I remember making an impact on me was the first of Eliot's 'Preludes' which I read in a school textbook when I was aged 13. I went to the library and found there were more preludes and more poems. I didn't understand a lot of what I read but I wanted to reproduce that kind of music, and that capacity to move the reader. I still feel very moved by the 'Preludes.'

I had stellar English teachers who taught me poetry at Friends Academy, a Quaker school on Long Island, but the first actual poet I studied with was W. N. Herbert at a summer programme in Oxford for American teenagers. I idolised Bill and returned to Long Island imitating his mannerisms minus the Scottish accent. I absentmindedly used his photo for a bookmark once and returned the book to the school library with his photo still inside. I was mortified when my English teacher, Mr Brogan, worked out it was me who last checked out that library book, and handed me back the photo with an impish twinkle.

The following summer I took a class with Mary Ruefle, then a professor at Bennington College who taught poetry to high school students in the summers. In addition to introducing me to Rilke and Gerard Manley Hopkins, she was refreshingly direct that I was writing some pretty bad poems, including a Stephen Crane imitation that had won me $300 in a dodgy vanity poetry competition.

So an early if unconventional British influence in Bill Herbert. I hadn't expected that. Later you studied with Kenneth Koch, one of the 'New York School' of poets. What did you learn from Koch?

I studied with Kenneth Koch at Colombia University. I learned everything from Koch. To whatever extent I idolised my former teachers, I idolised him still more: I went to every reading and talk he did like a crazed groupie, even for years after I graduated, until I moved to London.

The poets I looked at with him were Whitman, Dickinson, Hopkins, Rimbaud, Yeats, Stein, Rilke, Stevens, Apollinaire, Williams, Lawrence, Pound, Moore, Eliot (though I don't think Koch was a fan), Mayakowsky, Lorca, Auden, O'Hara and Ashbery.

Do you know his famous poem 'Variations on a Theme by William Carlos Williams'?

Yes, it's very clever, and funny.

He made us to do that kind of thing for homework all the time. Each time we studied a new poet, he required us to write an imitation. He'd read the best imitations out loud. Marianne Moore was the only poet I really managed to crack, and I nearly fainted when he read out my Moore imitation. Of my Apollinaire-inspired love caligramme, he said, 'That's not very passionate!'

I loved that he was urban, eccentric, mischievous, spacey and funny. He had a peculiar combination of guilelessness, irreverence and irony; one finds that combination in his poems too.

My favourite memory of him was when a student pointed out that a bird had made a nest on top of the chalk board in his lecture room. I guess a window was open, and – well – it was Manhattan, and we were far from Central Park. Not many places around to build nests. Koch, who was probably the opposite of a nature poet, said, 'What should we do? Help! Somebody call the biology department!' We laughed so hard we couldn't breathe. I still laugh to think of it.

One very good piece of advice he gave was 'If you feel you don't understand a poem, read everything by that poet.'

I don't hear much of an echo of Koch, Ashbery, O'Hara in your poetry—Louise Glück and Sylvia Plath seem more obvious influences. Who were your major role models?

Well I *feel* more closely aligned with the New York School than to Glück and Plath, but it's hard not to fall under Plath's spell, particularly as a female poet of my generation. She's one of those poets I have a visceral response to – which, for me, has nothing to do with subject matter but instead with music. Even when I have no idea what she's on about, like in 'Poppies in October', I'm under her spell. Not all of it, mind you, but much of it, certainly all of *Ariel*. Alice Oswald has that effect on me too. So do Eliot, Whitman, Hopkins, Rilke, Stevens and Berryman. I hear them and I go limp.

As for Glück, I had hoped to interview her in 2004. Although she didn't give interviews at that time, and perhaps still avoids them, she seemed on the brink of acquiescing, so I did weeks of research, read all her books, then read them all again. I came up with a list of questions that she generously deemed 'good questions', but she wouldn't go through with the interview. She did speak to me on the phone, though, for about an hour, answering the questions privately, with the understanding I not publish them. Given her anxieties about interviews, it was a kind gesture.

As my own first book was published in 2006, Glück's music must have attached itself to me, so to speak. And, anyway, how can a line like, 'At the end of my suffering there was a door' leave your head once it gets there? That hyper-lyrical voice-of-God kind of voice, that almost biblical voice, is so seductive to me.

You moved to London in 1999 though you visit the US regularly. How does British poetic practice differ from that in the US?

If by 'poetic practice' you mean 'aesthetics,' I actually tried to answer that question in an essay for *AGNI* magazine, published by Boston University, in 2008 when Maurice Riordan and I co-edited a 'British and Irish poetry supplement'. But seven years on, my answer would be completely different. Although historically there has been quite a lot of cross-cultural flow between British and American poetry, the two poetic worlds seemed hermetically sealed from each other when I first moved here. But now, once again, there's a great deal of communication between the poetic cultures. That said, most of it goes one way: British poets seem more interested in American poetry than the reverse, although editors like Don Share at *Poetry* in Chicago are doing their part to improve this. I find this American insularity deeply ironic given that England was the land of Chaucer, Wordsworth and Shakespeare.

Over the last 50 years American poetry seems to me to have been far more adventurous than British poetry – to have pushed the boundaries of form, addressing a wider canvas of concerns. Is that a fair judgement? How do you see the two traditions?

I think American poetry really started to push boundaries with the Modernists. So in my opinion it would actually be 100 years ago, not 50 years ago, when American poetry began to surpass British poetry in scope and freshness.

Yes I agree. I was just thinking of the more recent past.

You're right: 50 years ago one started to see a 'wider canvas of concerns', particularly with the so-called Confessional school, who tried to write 'authentically' and autobiographically in ways that were very direct and often unsettling.

Are the traditions moving closer? Kai Miller studied creative writing in the US before moving to Britain. Emily Berry and Luke Kennard are US influenced and Sam Riviere seems to deliberately write in a transatlantic style. Is British poetry becoming more 'American'?

I would say there is a noticeable US influence on some of the younger British voices that are getting attention now – the poets you mention for example. Of course there are diverse currents within contemporary poetry on both sides of the Atlantic and it's hard to generalise, and I can only talk about the poets whose work I know.

Roddy Lumsden deserves particular credit for introducing younger British writers to contemporary American poetry. He's taken a very active interest in what's happening in the States and, through his teaching here, has had considerable influence. He has introduced US poets liked Chelsey Minnis, Matthea Harvey, DA Powell, Brenda Shaugnessy, Noelle Kocot, Kathellen Ossip and Dorothea Lasky to a wider audience in Britain. Social media and the internet have also helped to reduce barriers to communication between the cultures.

I hear echoes of Jorie Graham in some of Alice Oswald's work.

I love thinking about poetic lineage – I'm always thinking about it – but I confess that you've stumped me with the Jorie Graham and Alice Oswald comparison! And I love that you stumped me; you've made me think. I suppose I see Graham as part of the Wallace Stevens lineage and Oswald, who, let's face it, mainly does her own thing, more of the Walt Whitman lineage, via Ted Hughes and, before him, D. H. Lawrence. Though I see Graham as part of the Stevens lineage, Graham nonetheless has that vastness on the page that recalls Whitman. So I think it's Whitman who probably links them. But Whitman links everyone. Whitman *is* everyone – or thought he was.

Yes I was thinking of the way both poets are able to bring the whole universe into a poem through focusing on something very specific – like Oswald's poem 'Field'. Maybe it's just that I've been reading both of them recently.

Whitman could be the link.

Your first collection *The Book of Jobs* was published in 2006, in New York. Do you see this as predominantly influenced by US poetic practice?

Yes. A number of the poems were written when I was getting my MA from Boston University.

Many of the poems deal with sadness, alienation, loss. 'Transference' for example starts 'I am a cold girl/I prefer a ghost in shoes to a man.' I think this is why I hear echoes of Plath's voice rather than Koch.

Yes, 'Transference' probably has a Plathian feel to it. It was written just after 9/11 when, coincidentally, I had been visiting New York with my son, then a toddler. I returned to London feeling both sad and anxious. In attempt to distract me, my husband took my son and me to Dover, where I projected dead bodies everywhere, even on the buoys in the sea. I didn't specifically reference the 9/11 context because I didn't think it was necessary.

In the poem 'The Factory' you talk about the moment you realised poetry was not 'dressing for dinner' but work. What is the background here?

That poem is a dialogue with myself. I work quite slowly. I imagined the Muse as a kind of production-line manager demanding output, and me in the factory trying on outfits rather than working.

Your second collection *God Loves You* was published here by Seren in 2013. I'm struck comparing the two volumes by the far greater degree of formal experimentation in the more recent book. There are prose poems, and epigrammatic forms sitting alongside quasi-sonnets. There's even a sestina. Did British poetry have any part in these stylistic developments?

Yes absolutely.

Say more.

In the US if someone writes a poem in unrhymed tercets, it's described as 'formal,' which is certainly not the case here, where 'formal' refers to the 'received forms.' Poetry written in traditional forms and metres is somewhat stigmatized in the States: it's seen as somewhat reactionary, which is of course ridiculous because you can infuse any form or style with energy and inventiveness. You don't seem to have that same kind of stigma here in the UK. British poetry makes more use of received form and often in interesting ways. In so many of Jamie McKendrick's poems, for example, the sonnet form is a kind of default. But then he tousles the form: clumsifies the metre and makes the rhymes sound like very distant music, hardly discernible. And there's a quasi villanelle, 'Unfaded', in *Crocodiles and Obelisks* where he has just one repeating line.

When I first moved here I confess I found a lot of British poetry very boring to read. British verse is generally quieter than American verse – less flashy. It took a while for my ear to become attuned to what was going on in the poems. Later I became fascinated by what poets like Alice Oswald, Nick Laird, Leontia Flynn, Michael Symmons Roberts, Jamie McKendrick and Simon Armitage were doing – poets whom Maurice and I included in our 2006 AGNI feature. The Flynn poem is a sestina. One of Jamie's pieces is a sonnet. So, yes, form started to interest me and, as you've already noted, some of the poems in *God Loves You* are written in received forms. That's a result of my moving here and not a development in my writing I had anticipated.

'Angel with Book' is I think a particularly beautiful poem. I love the idea of the angel keeping you out of the book by 'guile' and not recognising this as 'generosity'. What was the inspiration here?

Thank you. It was a sort of platonic love poem for a poet-friend, a love poem both to the poet and his poems. The 'angel' character – who I imagined to be a sort of anti angel of death – is such a stylised and abstracted version of my friend that it doesn't actually resemble him.

This is Jamie McKendrick, the dedicatee, presumably?

That's right. You can probably see Jamie's influence in my sonnets like 'Last Supper' or 'Lord Forgive Me.' The slightly dishevelled form is something

I learned partly from reading Jamie, although he's not the only poet who does it.

But the result doesn't sound 'British.'

I tried to project an American inflection into the poems, emulating someone like Frost. For example 'Will You Be My Friend, Kate Moss?' though written in blank verse, has a somewhat ditzy American speaker.

'The Sun's Lecture Notes on Itself, You and God' is another poem I admire. What was the genesis of this piece?

Simon Barraclough's solar-system class at the Poetry School. I thought that doing a course on the solar system might help with the God theme. In this exercise we had to write a poem from the perspective of the sun. This poem was a late inclusion in the book and in some ways represents a transition away from the other material. I wanted to try something in a fragmentary style.

The use of biblical analogies to provide a kind of linking thread through the collection is clever. At what point did this way of structuring the poems occur to you?

Very early on. All of my poems had the word God in them. It just kept reappearing. And I'm susceptible to certain registers of language. The King James Bible has a powerful and seductive register.

You're working on a third collection. What are your current preoccupations and influences? How do American and British traditions bear on your work now?

Recently someone introduced me at a reading as a 'disturbing poet'. I liked this description; it felt accurate because indeed my recent poems seem to be exploring dark, primal territory, aspects of ourselves that no one wants to talk about. I would say that these poems are neither particularly British nor particularly American. I think the two traditions are beginning to merge, and soon I expect it will be harder to distinguish between what is 'British' and what is 'American.' That's certainly true of my own work.

Kathryn Maris

School run

I board the same bus I boarded that morning
and see the same driver from the earlier journey.
Our eyes meet; he remembers me too.
When I exit, I feel abandoned by this driver

I know from those many morning journeys
to my daughter's school in northwest London.
Why do I feel the driver has abandoned me?
Has an imagined intimacy developed?

At my daughter's school in northwest London
were the usual mums and dads I greet
out of an imagined sense of intimacy
that has nothing to do with friendship.

Among the many mums and dads I greeted
out of politeness or something like fondness
that has nothing to do with friendship,
were business people and psychoanalysts.

Out of politeness or something like fondness,
I do not ask the driver why he left me.
He's not in the business of psychoanalysis;
it's not his job to say I miss my *daughter*,

that it was a loss when my daughter left
my body, when I met her eyes after her birth.
It is not his place to say I'm losing my daughter.
I exit the same bus I boarded that morning.

L'Enfer

As in life, she was a pain in the arse
in death too. He could hear her roaring
all the way from the fifth circle,
Why the hell do you get to be in a
better circle than me, I'm wrathful
because of your lust – A gust of wind
blew him to a different part of the
second circle where communication
with the fifth was impossible. A man
spoke to him commiseratively:
'We have to listen to those cows
for eternity. It's their moaning keeps
the furnaces lit.' He blew away again,
revelling in each brief moment of
freedom when the wind changed.
When there was time he wrote poems;
when he didn't have ideas he practised
writing in dialects he had little
familiarity with. Soon hell was filled
with his scribblings. wafting from circle
to circle in ascending order, then
burning in the furnace (which indeed
was fuelled by his wife) and wafting
again in their final form, ashes.

Ed Reiss

Zaffar Kunial, *Faber New Poets 11* (Faber and Faber, 2014)

This pamphlet is by the current Wordsworth Trust poet-in-residence. It is his first pamphlet and, according to the blurb on the back, until it he had published only one poem.

That poem, 'Hill Speak', a third prize-winner in the 2011 National Poetry Competition, contrasted the language of Kunial's father – 'Pahari-Potwari', a language with no written form – with the poet's own language: English. Issues of identity are raised in this pamphlet's beginning poem, 'The Word', in which the non-native father misuses the definite article in his advice to 'enjoy the life'. Again the wider question of biculturalism is addressed through the minute particulars of language. Zaffar Kunial is writing in a Romantic tradition of self-examination and self-accusation ('Ashamed. Aware.'). He is in 'a halfway house', 'half right, half/ wrong' and that symptomatic word 'half' will be repeated in 'half-opened' (p. 7), 'half a mind' (p. 10), 'Half cast' and 'cast / half' (p. 13).

The collection's second poem refers to Wordsworth's revisions in *The Prelude* of his passage about leaving the tumultuous throng of fellow skaters 'to cut across the shadow of a star'. 'Shadow' is the wrong word, so Wordsworth changed it to 'image', then later to 'reflex'. When Seamus Heaney wrote about this (in 'Wordsworth's Skates', in *District and Circle)*, the Irish poet slipped up, locating Wordsworth's poem on Windermere instead of Esthwaite. Kunial writes about accuracy and self-correction, the skates, ice and star, once again scored in the 'sliding place' of language.

These are poems about people and feelings, which sketch a story of relationships and relationships gone wrong. The poems contain emotion, particularly pain, in the sense that they are both emotional and restrained. At the same time, they refer to literary provenance with echoes and allusions which open deeper spaces of intertextuality. Although the voice is quiet, the aim is ambitious and accomplished, with references to Donne and Dickens, as well as Einstein 'wedding time and space' (p. 11). Among more recent writers there may be stylistic traces of Michael Donaghy, Paul Muldoon, Don Paterson, Carol Ann Duffy and Paul Farley.

This is partly a matter of formal invention, for one of the strengths of this collection is its inventive handling of form. The poems about relationships (poet, partner, child) are written as tercets ('And Farther Again', 'Us'). Muldoonian rhymed haikus look at other relationships (including poet, mother, father). There are a couple of Shakespearean sonnets ('The Word',

'Spider Trees, Pakistan'); an upside down sonnet ('The Lyric Eye'); a defective sonnet ('On the Brief'); a sonnet with a quatrain inserted ('Placeholder'); and a quirkily-rhymed sonnet ('Q').

A successful collection must blend unity with surprise. In this case some sense of unity is achieved by repetition across the collection of 'heart words' such as 'between'. So the pamphlet begins with the definite article misplaced 'between enjoy and life'. 'Empty Words' is concerned with what is 'between written and oral' (p. 6) and 'between / the p and the t' of that word 'empty' (p. 7). Elsewhere Kunial is stuck between the workaday world and the Wordsworthian sublime, 'between nine-to-five and spots of time; / the stars snowing through the screensaver // and the rain-clotted window' (p. 10). He is stranded 'between love // and loss' (p. 12). And he is only here because his mother met his 'eventual father' on a wander 'between trains' (p. 17). Other key words threading the collection together include 'back', 'door', 'eyes', 'hand', 'here', 'home', 'nail', 'now', 'script', 'star' and 'wave'. This core vocabulary means that whilst each poem creates its own lexis and establishes its own terms, each also invokes others, creating a whole greater than the sum of its parts.

The surprise in this collection partly stems from subject-matter: Mexican waves, international debt, Archimedes. A single poem moves from a hieroglyph of the Sui Dynasty, through thirteenth century Iran to rejection in the aftermath of splitting up. There is also surprise in the language: so the 'well-thumbed' light in a dim pub is not vague or misty but 'particular as fog', suggesting perhaps an idea of fog as individual particles. In 'Fielder' the light has 'slipped the dark cordon of rhododendron hands', playing on the idea of a cordon of slip-fielders.

All but one poem includes the word 'I' and this 'I' usually exists and acts in the present tense of the poem, often as the writer struggling for the right word. The main mimesis then is directed towards showing the mind's self-experience in the act of thinking.

In his 'Table Talk' Coleridge notes how one sentence in Shakespeare "begets the next naturally; the meaning is all interwoven. He goes on kindling like a meteor through the dark atmosphere." At this collection's close, 'A Drink at the Door', the glow round the poet's pew 'hosts its own table talk' as he sits alone reading from his Kindle. Sure enough, that word 'Kindle' begets the internal half-rhyme of the verb 'candles'. A pub called 'The Bear' leads us to 'burr' in the sense of prickly seed-vessel, then through 'bitter' (adjective not noun) and 'bear' (as verb) to 'burr' in the sense of dialectal rough uvular trill. This closing poem covers 190 years and a mass of 'dark matter' with verve and care.

If there is one rhetorical figure which characterises this booklet as a whole, it might be adynaton: the figure which declares inability to describe something adequately. So the collection begins with 'I couldn't tell you now', a figure repeated in the third poem with 'I can't put into words'. Adynaton often includes a paradox in that the very expression of inadequacy conveys something of what one wishes to communicate. ("I can't tell you how much I like this collection!" tells you something of how much I like it.) So the final couplet of one sonnet finds Kunial looking at photos on a webpage, 'racking my brain for lines to catch how they carry / the gravities of home. Worlds I can't marry.' That profession of failure is balanced and belied by the rhyme, which effects a kind of marriage at the auditory level as 'carry' marries 'marry'.

As a reviewer I too feel adynaton in that I can't sufficiently describe the excellence of this collection. So consider in full a short lyric, 'Butterfly Soup', which draws on catastrophe theory; which is metaphysical in several senses (addressing the nature of Being, relating to the transcendent, yoking heterogeneous ideas together); and which conceives of poetry as metaphor and metamorphosis, as flower, butterfly and universe. It does all this with wit and humour. Note the play of 'this' and 'that' and in the final line that transitive use of the verb 'flaps': right for a butterfly's beating wings, but also perhaps suggesting comically minor agitation, a storm in a teacup.

> This butterfly comes from a bud
> they call the small cocoon
> it occupied before it was
> this speckled, flitting bloom.
>
> Back in that darkly shrunken space
> it breaks down cell by cell.
> Now, liquefied, its black-holed eyes
> gape past that pupal gel:
>
> that dense and nascent universe
> that spooled our sent-out star.
> This point that bore that point before
>
> flaps storms to Palomar.

Biographies

David Ball lives in Besançon, and has been published in a variety of magazines. He would like to be noted for juxtaposing different styles, themes and voices, often within the same poem.

Jonathan Barker has edited bibliographies of contemporary poetry, an edition of the poems of W. H. Davies and co-edited an edition of the *Collected Poems and Selected* Translations of Norman Cameron. His recent research has been on R. W. Dixon and D. G. Rossetti.

William Bedford's selected poems, *Collecting Bottles Tops*, and selected short stories, *None of the Cadillacs Was Pink*, were both published in 2009. A new collection of poems, *The Fen Dancing*, was published in the spring of 2014. His poem 'Then' won First Prize in the 2014 Roundel Poetry Competition. His poem 'The Journey' won First Prize in the 2014 *London Magazine* International Poetry Competition.

Martin Bennett lives in Rome where he teaches and proofreads at the University of tor Vergata. He was this year's winner of the John Clare Poetry Prize.

Diana Brodie was born in New Zealand but emigrated to the United Kingdom in 1966 and settled in Cambridge. Three decades later, she wrote her first poem. Her work has been published in four countries in many journals and anthologies, in *Rialto, Agenda, Poetry Salzburg Review* and *Poetry News*. Her collection, *Giotto's Circle,* was published by Poetry Salzburg n 2013.

Lia Brooks is 37 years old and has worked for many years in the care sector. Her poetry has been twice nominated for the Pushcart Prize and has been published in various magazines and journals in the UK and the US, some of which include; *Poetry London*, *Lily Lit Review*, *California Quarterly*, *Mslexia*, *Magma Poetry* newsletters, *Qarrtsiluni*, *American Poetry Journal*, *Loch Raven Review*, *Penumbra*. She was short-listed for the New Leaf Short Poetry Prize and was a prizewinner in the Troubadour Poetry Prize. She has been part of three ekphrastic events in collaboration with painters in Indiana and California. She was born in Epsom, Surrey, and lives in Southampton, UK, with her partner and two sons.

Simon Collings lives in Oxford, UK. He has worked in international development for 25 years and was Fundraising Director of Oxfam for six years. Simon has published poems in a number of journals and ezines including *The Interpreters' House, Ink, Sweat & Tears,* and *Sentinel Literary Quarterly*. He has two poems in issue 10 of *New Walk.*

David Cooke's retrospective collection, *In the Distance,* was published in 2011 by Night Publishing. A new collection, *Work Horses,* was published by Ward Wood in 2012. His poems and reviews have appeared in journals such as *Agenda, The Bow Wow Shop, The Interpreter's House, The Irish Press, The London Magazine, Magma, The Morning Star, New Walk, The North, Poetry Ireland Review, Poetry Salzburg Review, The Reader, The SHOp* and *Stand*. He has two collections forthcoming: *A Murmuration* (Two Rivers Press, 2015) and *After Hours* (Cultured Llama Pres 2017).

Angela Croft spent her childhood split between London, Wales and Cornwall. A journalist and Government Press Officer she took to writing poetry in retirement, and has been widely published and is one of six poets to have a collection in *Caboodle* launched by Prolebooks (in March).

Tony Curtis was born in Dublin in 1955. An award-winning poet, Curtis has published nine warmly received collections. His most recent collections are: *Pony* (with paintings and drawing by David Lilburn, Occasional Press 2013); *Currach* (with photographs by Liam Blake, 2013); *Folk* (Arc Publications 2011). His children's book *An Elephant Called Rex and a Dog Called Dumbo* (with illustrations by Pat Mooney) was published in 2011. A new collection *Approximately in the Key of C* is forthcoming from Arc Publications. Curtis has been awarded the Varuna House exchange Fellowship to Australia, The Irish National Poetry Prize, and has read his poetry all over the world. He is a member of Aosdana.

John Gladwell lives on the North Essex coast and has work published in a variety of magazines including *PN Review, London Magazine, The Rialto, Stand, Ambit* and previous issues of *Agenda*.

Kate Hendry teaches English at Edinburgh Napier University. She was recently the reader in residence at the National Library of Scotland. Her poetry, short fiction and non fiction have been published in a number of magazines and anthologies, including *New Writing Scotland*, the Bridport Prize 2009 anthology, *Harpers*, *Mslexia*, *Northwords Now*, *The Red Wheelbarrow*, *The Reader* and *The Rialto*.

Stuart Henson's fourth collection *The Odin Stone* was published by Shoestring Press in 2011. The poems in this issue are from a collaboration with artist Bill Sanderson exploring the world of medieval misericords — due from Shoestring later in 2015.

Eleanor Hooker is an Irish poet, her first collection of poems, *The Shadow Owner's Companion* (The Dedalus Press) was shortlisted for best first collection 2012. Eleanor is currently completing her second collection of poems.

Roland John has had a long association with *Agenda*. Agenda Editions published his first full collection *Believing Words are Real* in 1985. He has written many articles and essays on Ezra Pound, his *A Beginner's Guide to The Cantos of Ezra Pound* examines each canto in detail. His latest poetry collection is *A Lament for England*. He is currently working on a new collection.

Jeffrey Joseph was born in London in 1952 and was educated at The University of York, University College, Cardiff and at The Open University. He lectures at Trinity Laban Conservatoire of Music and Dance and elsewhere and is a regularly performed composer. He has written about music for most of the leading specialist periodicals and his poetry has been published in various magazines such as *Fire*, *Anon* and *Borderlines*.

Noel King was born and lives in Tralee. His poems, haiku, short stories, reviews and articles have appeared in magazines and journals in thirty-seven countries. His poetry collections are published by Salmon Poetry: *Prophesying the Past*, (2010), *The Stern Wave* (2013) and *Sons* (forthcoming in 2015). He has edited more than fifty books of work by others. Anthology publications include *The Second Genesis: An Anthology of Contemporary World Poetry*

Gill Learner lives in Reading. Her poems have been widely published in journals such as *Acumen*, *Mslexia*, *Poetry News* and *Smiths Knoll*, and a variety of anthologies. It has also won a number of awards including the Poetry Society's Hamish Canham Prize 2008 and the English Association's Fellows' Poetry Prize 2012. Her first collection, *The Agister's Experiment*, was published by Two Rivers Press in 2011. She reads regularly at Reading's Poets' Café.

Jane Lovell runs the Warwickshire Poetry Stanza for the Poetry Society and her poems have appeared in a range of publications and anthologies including *Poetry Wales, New Welsh Review, Myslexia, Envoi*, webzine *Ink, Sweat & Tears* and *Poetry News*. She is a regular contributor to *Agenda*.

Dan MacIsaac writes from Vancouver Island. In 2014, he received the Foley Poetry Award from *America Magazine*. His poetry has appeared in many journals, including, in 2013 and 2014, the print magazines *Poetica*, *Vallum*, *Poetry Salzburg* and *Agenda*. Links to publications of his verse by journals online, such as at http://www.contemporaryverse2.ca/en/poetry/excerpt/ode-to-ee, can be found on the publications page of his website, danmacisaac.com. His fiction appeared in a recent issue of *Stand* and is forthcoming in *Brittle Star*.

Sue Mackrell teaches Creative Writing at Loughborough University. Her poetry and short stories have been published in anthologies and magazines including *Agenda, Riptide,* and *The Coffee House*, and in a poetry collection, *Rhythms*. She is co-director of Crystal Clear Creators, a not for profit organisation committed to promoting new writing. Current projects include an Arts Council project writing a short play based on Lutterworth Workhouse, and a Heritage Lottery funded project exploring 'untold stories' of the Home Front in Leicester during the First World War, including Music Halls, and the experiences of local conscientious objectors.

Terry McDonagh www.t-online.de writes for adults and children. He has held residencies in Europe, Asia and Australia. He has published eight poetry collections, a book of letters, as well as prose and poetry for young people. Translated into Indonesian and German and distributed internationally by Syracuse Uni. Press. His latest children's story, *Michel the Merman*, illustrated by Marc Barnes (NZ), was published in Hamburg in autumn 2013. He has just completed, *Echolocation*, poetry for young people. He lives in Ireland and Hamburg.

Gill McEvoy has had two collections from Cinnamon Press *The Plucking Shed* (2010), and *Rise* (2013). *The First Telling*, Happenstance Press, 2014. Gill collaborates with singer Polly Bolton to produce 'sung and read' shows, and this year *Out of the Land* will be performed around Shropshire .She runs several regular poetry events in Chester where she lives, from workshops to poetry reading groups. She is a 2012 Hawthornden Fellow.

Hugh McMillan is a poet from South West Scotland, an award winner in several competitions including the Smith/Doorstep Pamphlet Prize, the Callum MacDonald Prize and the Cardiff International Poetry Competition. He has been published and anthologised widely. His latest book *The Other Creatures in the Wood* has just been published by Mariscat. He has just finished a book on contemporary visions of Dumfries and Galloway, commissioned by the Wigtown Book Festival.

W S Milne, Scottish poet, dramatist and critic has just completed a translation of the *Iliad* into Scots. His most recent essay was a review of Samuel Beckett's *Letters* in *The London Magazine*.

Ralph Monday is an Associate Professor of English at Roane State Community College in Harriman, TN., where he teaches composition, literature, and creative writing courses. He has been published widely in over 50 journals including *The New Plains Review, New Liberties Review, Fiction Week Literary Review and many others*. His poetry has been nominated for a Pushcart Prize and Houghton Mifflin's "Best of" Anthologies, as well as other awards. A chapbook, *All American Girl and Other Poems*, was published in July 2014. A book *Lost Houses and American Renditions* is scheduled for publication in May 2015 by Aldrich Press.

Paul Murray was born in Dublin in 1954. His poetry has appeared in the *Poetry Ireland Review* and he has written school text books in the Irish language. He teaches in Oatlands College, Mount Merrion.

Jessamine O'Connor's chapbooks *Hellsteeth* and *A Skyful of Kites*, are available from www.jessamineoconnor.com. Facilitator of the *Wrong Side of the Tracks Writers,* and director of poetry/art/music ensemble *The Hermit Collective,* she has won the *Yeats* and *Francis Ledwidge* awards, and been widely published, most recently in *Tridae; Poetry NZ; Skylight47; The Colour of Saying,* and forthcoming in *Yeats150*.

Richard Ormrod is a biographer, journalist, and sometime OU tutor in Creative Writing. He is working towards his first collection. He is also currently writing the authorised critical biography of the poet Andrew Young.

Stuart A Paterson was born in 1966 and raised in Ayrshire, Scotland, in a Scots-speaking household. From 1989 until 1996 he founded and edited the international poetry and prose review *Spectrum*. In 1992 he was awarded an Eric Gregory Award from the Society of Authors. In 2014 he was awarded a Robert Louis Stevenson Fellowship from the Scottish Book Trust. Saving Graces was published by diehard in 1997. His work has been widely published and anthologised in the UK and overseas.

Mario Petrucci is a multi-award-winning poet and residency frontiersman, the only poet to have held residencies at the Imperial War Museum and with BBC Radio 3. 'Reminiscent of e.e. cummings at his best' (*Envoi*), Petrucci aspires to 'Poetry on a geological scale' (*Verse*). *i tulips* (Enitharmon, 2010) takes its name from Petrucci's vast Anglo-American sequence, whose 'modernist marvels' (*Poetry Book Society*) convey his distinctive combination of innovation and humanity. www.mariopetrucci.com

David Pollard was born under the bed in 1942 and has been furniture salesman, accountant, TEFL teacher and university lecturer. He got his three degrees from the University of Sussex and has since taught at the universities of Sussex, Essex and the Hebrew University of Jerusalem. He has published *The Poetry of Keats: Language and Experience* which was his doctoral thesis, *A KWIC Concordance to the Harvard Edition of Keats' Letters*, a novel, *Nietzsche's Footfalls,* and four volumes of poetry, *patricides*, *Risk of Skin*, *bedbound* and *Self-Portraits*. He has also been published in other volumes and in learned journals and poetry magazines.

Caroline Price is a violinist and teacher living in Tunbridge Wells, where she also helps to run the Kent & Sussex Poetry Society. Her short stories have been shortlisted for both the Bridport and Asham awards, and she has published three collections of poetry, most recently *Wishbone* (Shoestring Press 2008).

Ed Reiss lives and works in Bradford. He has written *Now then* (2006) and *Your sort* (2011), both published by Smith/Doorstop, Sheffield.

James Roberts lives in Wales. Recent poetry and essays have appeared in *Agenda*, *Envoi*, *The Clearing* and *Earthlines*. A small collection of 15 poems will be published by Cinnamon Press in August.

Robyn Rowland lives in Australia and Ireland. She has six books of poetry, and two CDs: *Off the tongue* and *Silver Leaving - Poems & Harp* with Irish harpist Lynn Saoirse. *Seasons of doubt & burning. New & Selected Poems* (2010) represents 40 years of poetry. Her work appears in *Being Human*, ed. Neil Astley, (Bloodaxe Books, 2011). She has read, and been published, in many countries including Turkey, Portugal, India, Austria, Bosnia, Serbia. Honorary Fellow, School of Culture & Communication, Melbourne University. She is currently working on a bi-lingual book with Dr Mehmet Ali Çelikel .

Julie-ann Rowell's first pamphlet collection, *Convergence*, published by Brodie Press, won a Poetry Book Society Award. Her first full collection, *Letters North*, was nominated for the Michael Murphy Poetry Prize for Best First Collection in Britain and Ireland in 2011. She has been teaching poetry in Bristol for eight years.

Omar Sabbagh is a widely published poet and critic. His three extant poetry collections include: *My Only Ever Oedipal Complaint* and *The Square Root of Beirut* (Cinnamon Press, 2010/12). A fourth collection: *To The Middle Of Love*, is forthcoming with Cinnamon Press in late 2016. In January 2014 Rodopi published his monograph: *From Sight through to In-Sight: Time, Narrative and Subjectivity in Conrad and Ford*. He also has a novella set in and about Beirut, *Via Negativa*, forthcoming with Cinnamon Press's new Imprint, *Liquorice Fish*, at the start of 2016. He has published essays on George Eliot, Ford Madox Ford, Joseph Conrad, Lawrence Durrell, G.K. Chesterton, Henry Miller, Robert Browning, and many contemporary poets. He is currently Assistant Professor in English at the American University in Dubai (AUD). Website: www.omarsabbagh.me

Born in 1948 **Bill Sanderson** went to art school in Bristol and has been a freelance illustrator since the early 1970s. His work has appeared in magazines, books and advertisements, all employing the medium of scraperboard. His initial editorial commissions were mainly for UK magazines and newspapers including *The Times*, *New Scientist* and *The Radio Times*. He also had many years drawing for the American edition of *Esquire*. In 2005 he won the V&A Book Cover and Jacket Illustration Award with Steve Snider the designer, for *The Preservationist* by David Maine.

Caroline Smith has published two poetry books with Flambard Press. *Flambard New Poets1* and *Thistles of the Hesperides*. She is currently finishing her new collection, *The Immigration Handbook*. Her poems have been widely published in journals including the Bloodaxe anthology *Staying Alive*. Her poetry has been set to music and performed by the BBC Singers on Radio 3. In 2012 and 2013 she was a prize-winner in the Troubadour Poetry Competition. She works as the Immigration and Asylum caseworker for a London MP.

Will Stone is a poet, essayist and literary translator who divides his time between Suffolk, North Devon and the European outlands. His first poetry collection *Glaciation* (Salt, 2007), won the international Glen Dimplex Award for poetry in 2008. A second collection *Drawing in Ash*, was published by Salt in May 2011. His next collection *The Sleepwalkers* will appear in 2015/16. His translated works include *To the Silenced – Selected Poems of Georg Trakl* Arc, (2005) and more recently a series of books for Hesperus Press, with translations of works by Maurice Betz, Stefan Zweig, Joseph Roth and Rainer Maria Rilke. Arc will publish his two collections of translated poetry by Belgian symbolist poets Emile Verhaeren and Georges Rodenbach in 2015. Further translations of essays by Stefan Zweig will appear from Pushkin Press in 2015/16 and a *Collected Poems of Georg Trakl* will be published by Seagull Books in 2016.

Howard Wright lectures in Art History at the Belfast School of Art. Blackstaff Press published *King of Country* in 2010 which was shortlisted for the London New Fringe Poetry Award. Templar Press/ Iota shots followed this with *Blue Murder* in 2011. He won the 2012 Bedford Open Poetry prize. New poems are due to be published in *Cyphers*, *Dark Horse* and *The Antigonish Review*.

PN Review

'The most engaged, challenging and serious-minded of all the UK's poetry magazines.'
- Simon Armitage

- Letters
- News and Notes
- Articles
- Interviews
- Reviews
- Features
- Poems

Previous issues have featured major poets *Andrew Motion, Sophie Hannah, Sinead Morrissey, Elaine Feinstein, John Ashbery, Sujata Bhatt, Edwin Morgan, Eavan Boland, Les Murray* and others.

'Bracing.'
- The Independent

Subscribe to PN *Review* at
www.pnreview.co.uk